A Slice of Kentucky

Sharing Our Recipes

McClanahan
Publishing House

International Standard Book Number 0-913383 87-2
Library of Congress Card Catalog Number 2003110846

Cover design and book layout by James Asher Graphics
Photographs by James Asher

Manufactured in the United States of America

All book order correspondence should be addressed to:

McClanahan Publishing House, Inc.
P. O. Box 100
Kuttawa, KY 42055

1-800-544-6959

www.kybooks.com
books@kybooks.com

Table of Contents

Acknowledgments

Our Friends and Families
Kentucky Dining by the Lakes by Meredith Eddy and Paula Cunningham
American Sampler by Linda Bauer
The Cunningham Family Cookbook by the Cunningham Cousins
Simply Tennessee by Betty Jane McClanahan
Merry Christmas from Tennessee by Betty Jane McClanahan
Delicious and Deliteful by Verne Louise Dobbs
Derby Entertaining
Nuts about Pecans by Edna Trull
Merry Christmas from Kentucky by Michelle Stone
Merry Christmas from the South by Michelle Stone
Merry Christmas from Georgia by Michelle Stone
Soccer Mom Cookbook
Merry Christmas from Texas by Katherine Helms
Kentucky Always in Season by Greta Hipp Burkhart
Savor Superior by Judy Kreag
Seasoned in the South by Susanne Arthur
South Carolina Always in Season by Ann Burger
Fancy to Down Home by Sherrie Penn

Preface

A Slice of Kentucky, is just what it says. It's slices of recipe collections drawn from our ever-widening circle of friends.

Yes, we're known as the "cookbook ladies," although we have published more than just recipe books in the last 20 years. Wherever and whenever we travel to trade shows and pass out food samples, people always comment, "Oh, you're the cookbook ladies!" So over the years we've become known as just that. And, we love it.

We all enjoy cooking, dining in great restaurants, sampling a chef's wares directly from his kitchen stock pots, or sharing the newest, easiest recipes we've ever discovered. This collection offers up our favorites!

Of course we don't claim to have all original recipes. Who does? Not too many folks. And the best recipes, of course, are the ones passed from friend to friend or family to family.

So it is with *A Slice of Kentucky, Sharing Our Recipes*. We've borrowed our very favorite recipes from some of our very favorite authors and cooks. We like the quick and easy recipes, no doubt about it—who wouldn't? We are all working and taking care of families, managing our jobs and doing all of the volunteer stuff that goes along with the Kentucky woman's role.

We've also offered some sample menus to help you plan ahead. We hope these will spark your creative juices and get you excited about entertaining. Sometimes we all just need a push.

A warm thanks to all who have shared their recipes for this book. We hope you enjoy *A Slice of Kentucky* and recommend it to your friends and family.

As Thomas Wolfe so eloquently stated, "There is no spectacle on earth more appealing than that of a beautiful woman in the act of cooking dinner for someone she loves."

The Cookbook Ladies

Beginnings & Beverages

Preservation Kentucky
Afternoon Reception

Cheesy Bacon Ball, page 11

Mushroom Croustades, page 14

Country Ham Balls, page 16

Vegetable Tray with Spicy Horseradish Dip, page 20

Kentucky Chocolate Bourbon Balls, page 152

Chocolate Mint Kisses, page 152

Cranberry-Zinfandel Punch, page 29

At spring wedding showers and graduation get-togethers, creamy rounds of Brie cheese baked in a golden pastry make beautiful additions to the table.

Baked Brie with Chives

Pastry dough for a 9-inch pie
8-ounce wheel Brie cheese, thoroughly chilled
1 large egg, beaten with 1 tablespoon water
1 to 1½ tablespoons snipped fresh chives

Roll the pastry dough to ⅛ inch thickness. Cut two circles from the dough – one 7 inches in diameter and one 3 inches in diameter. Place the Brie in the middle of the larger circle and fold the pastry up, wrapping the cheese and pleating the pastry up snugly over the sides and the rim of the cheese. Brush the pastry on top with a small amount of the beaten egg. Sprinkle the chives evenly over the exposed cheese. Place the small circle of pastry on top of the cheese, pressing down at the edges to seal the cheese completely inside. Brush the top of the pastry with some of the egg. Make small decorative cutouts from the remaining scraps of dough and arrange them on top of the pastry, brushing the cutouts with the egg. Place on a baking sheet and bake at 400 degrees for 20 minutes or until the pastry is golden and crisp. Remove from the oven and allow the cheese to cool for 15 minutes. Place the pastry on a serving plate and slice it into wedges before serving.

Makes 4 to 6 appetizer servings.

Charmin' Cherry Cheese Ball

½ cup butter, at room temperature
1 cup grated Cheddar cheese
8-ounce package cream cheese, at room temperature
3 green onions, chopped
1 cup real bacon bits
12-ounce jar cherry preserves

Combine the butter, Cheddar cheese and cream cheese. Shape the mixture into a ball. Roll the ball in the onions and bacon bits; chill. Chop the preserves in a blender container for a few seconds. Pour the preserves over the ball and serve with crackers.

Cheesy Bacon Ball

8 ounces sharp shredded Cheddar cheese, at room temperature
8 ounces mayonnaise
1 bunch green onions, chopped
1 pound crispy fried bacon, drained and crumbled
Parsley

Combine the cheese and mayonnaise in a large bowl and mix well. Add the onions and bacon and mix well. Cover and chill. Remove the cheese mixture from the refrigerator and form into 1 large ball or 2 small balls. Garnish with the parsley or roll in chopped parsley before serving.

Pineapple Cheese Ball

16 ounces cream cheese, at room temperature
8-ounce can crushed pineapple, drained
½ green pepper, chopped
2 tablespoons chopped onion
1 teaspoon salt
1 cup crushed pecans

Combine the cream cheese and pineapple; mix well. Add the green pepper, onion and salt; mix well. Cover and chill. Remove from the refrigerator and shape into 1 large ball. Roll the ball in the crushed pecans. Chill until ready to serve.

Baked Gouda

8-ounce package crescent rolls
1 small round gouda cheese

Separate the crescent rolls. Place the rolls on a baking sheet with the points out making a circle. Remove the wax from the cheese and place in the center of the circle. Pull up the points of the rolls until the cheese is covered. Press the seams together to seal and bake according to the crescent roll package directions. Allow the cheese to stand for 5 minutes before transferring to a serving tray.

Serves 4.

Sensational Sausage Appetizer

1 pound pork sausage
½ pound chopped, fresh mushrooms
1 pound Velveeta cheese, cubed
3 tablespoons creamy Italian dressing
Salt and pepper to taste
Party rye bread slices

Brown the sausage in a skillet; drain and set aside. Sauté the mushrooms in the skillet; drain. Combine the sausage and mushrooms. Melt the cheese in a small bowl in the microwave. Add the cheese and dressing to the sausage mixture. Season with the salt and pepper; mix well. Place the mixture on the party rye bread slices and broil in the oven until brown. Serve hot.

Great starter! Try this instead of the usual sausage balls.

This recipe freezes well.

Mushroom Croustades

24 slices white bread, very thinly sliced
Soft butter
4 tablespoons butter
3 tablespoons finely-chopped green onions
½ pound mushrooms, chopped
2 tablespoons flour
1 cup heavy cream
½ teaspoon salt
¼ teaspoon cayenne pepper
1 tablespoon finely-chopped chives
½ teaspoon lemon juice
2 tablespoons Parmesan cheese

Cut one round from each slice of bread with a 3-inch cookie cutter. Coat each round heavily with the soft butter. Fit the rounds into tiny muffin cups. Bake at 400 degrees for 10 minutes. Do not overcook.

Heat the 4 tablespoons of butter in a skillet until the foam subsides. Add the onions and sauté for 4 minutes. Add the mushrooms and cook until done. Remove the skillet from the heat and sprinkle in the flour; stir. Add the cream. Return the skillet to the heat and bring to a boil. Reduce the heat and simmer for 1 minute. Add the salt, cayenne pepper, chives and lemon juice. Pour the mixture into a bowl and chill for 30 minutes. Spoon the mixture into the rounds. Sprinkle with the Parmesan cheese and dot with butter. Bake at 350 degrees for 10 minutes.

Serves 8 to 12.

Little Oyster Pies

½ cup butter
6 ounces cream cheese, at room temperature
¾ cup flour
1 tablespoon cold water
Three 3¾-ounce cans smoked oysters, drained

Cut the butter and cream cheese into the flour in a mixing bowl. Add the water; chill. Roll the chilled dough on a well-floured board to ⅛-inch thick; cut 36 rounds with a biscuit cutter. Place the smoked oysters on half of each round; fold over and seal edges with fork, prick the top. Bake at 450 degrees for 20 to 30 minutes.

Makes 36 appetizers.

Tailgating Pretzels

13.5-ounce box Snyder's hanover-style pretzels
1 stick butter
1 cup vegetable or canola oil
1-ounce envelope onion soup mix

Break the pretzels into bite-size pieces. Melt the butter; add the oil and onion soup mix. Add the pretzel pieces and stir until well coated. Spread the pretzels evenly onto a baking sheet. Bake at 250 degrees for 1½ hours or until the soup mixture has been absorbed. Let the pretzels cool and enjoy!

A snacking favorite! Tasty munchies for those sporting events and other get-togethers.

Country Ham Balls

1 pound ground, cooked country ham
½ pound sausage
½ cup dry bread crumbs
1 egg
Milk
2 cups brown sugar
1 tablespoon prepared mustard
1 cup water
1 cup vinegar

Combine the ham, sausage, bread crumbs and egg; mix well. Add enough of the milk to roll the mixture into small balls. Place the balls in a coated 9x13-inch baking dish. Combine the brown sugar, mustard, water and vinegar in a saucepan and bring the mixture to a boil. Pour ½ of the sauce over the balls. Bake at 400 degrees for 45 minutes or until firm. Pour the remaining sauce over the balls when serving.

Sausage Balls

1 pound pork sausage
1 egg, beaten
⅓ cup bread stuffing
¼ cup ketchup
¼ cup chili sauce
1 tablespoon soy sauce
1 tablespoon vinegar
2 tablespoons brown sugar
½ cup water

Combine the sausage, egg and stuffing in a bowl; mix well. Form the mixture into balls. Brown the balls in a skillet and drain. Add the ketchup, chili sauce, soy sauce, vinegar, brown sugar and water. Return the balls to the skillet and simmer for 30 minutes. Chill or freeze. Reheat the balls and place them in a chafing dish when ready to serve.

Derby Afternoon Cheese Straws

½ **pound grated extra-sharp Cheddar cheese**
¼ **pound softened butter**
½ **teaspoon salt**
⅛ **teaspoon cayenne pepper**
1½ **cups flour**
Paprika
Salt

Combine the cheese, butter, salt, cayenne pepper and flour in a bowl; mix into a soft, pliable dough. Add a few drops of water if needed. Roll the dough on a lightly floured board. Cut the dough into straws using a sharp knife or pizza cutter. Place the straws on an uncoated baking sheet. Bake at 325 degrees for 20 minutes or until the straws begin to lightly brown around the edges. Allow to cool. Sprinkle the straws lightly with the paprika and salt. Store in an airtight container between sheets of waxed paper.

Makes 6 dozen straws.

A favorite snack for that famous Kentucky race!

Crab Dip

Two 8-ounce packages cream cheese, at room temperature
⅓ cup mayonnaise
1 tablespoon powdered sugar
1 tablespoon dry white wine
½ teaspoon minced onion
½ teaspoon prepared mustard
¾ teaspoon garlic salt
¼ teaspoon salt
1 cup fresh crab meat
Chopped fresh parsley

Combine the cream cheese, mayonnaise and powdered sugar in a bowl; mix well. Add the wine, onion, mustard, garlic salt and salt; mix well. Add the crab meat, stirring gently. Spoon the mixture into a coated 1-quart baking dish. Bake at 375 degrees for 15 minutes. Remove from the oven and sprinkle with the parsley. Serve warm with assorted crackers.

Makes about 2¾ cups.

Chilled Crab Dip

8-ounce package cream cheese, at room temperature
½ cup mayonnaise
¼ cup finely-grated Cheddar cheese
1 small garlic clove, pressed
1 teaspoon Worcestershire sauce
Salt and freshly-ground black pepper to taste
1 cup fresh crab meat, shredded

Combine the cream cheese and mayonnaise in a mixing bowl and beat with an electric mixer. Add the cheese, garlic, Worcestershire sauce, salt, pepper and crab meat; mix well. Chill until ready to serve. Serve with assorted crackers.

Makes approximately 1 cup.

Clam Dip

8-ounce package cream cheese
6½-ounce can clams, drained, reserving juice
2 tablespoons Worcestershire sauce
Dash of salt

Combine the cream cheese and reserved clam juice in a bowl until it is a smooth, thick consistency. Add the Worcestershire sauce, clams and salt. Mix well and chill.

Shrimp Dip

10¾-ounce can tomato soup
8 ounces cream cheese
1 cup mayonnaise
1 cup diced celery
¼ cup diced onion
2 cups shrimp, fresh or canned
1 teaspoon Worcestershire sauce
Dash of garlic powder

Heat the tomato soup in a small saucepan. Add the cream cheese and beat until smooth. Add the mayonnaise, celery, onion, shrimp, Worcestershire sauce and garlic powder; mix well. Pour the mixture into a serving dish, cover and chill until ready to serve.

Combine 1 teaspoon unflavored gelatin and 1/2 cup of water for a molded dish. Add the gelatin mixture to the cheese mixture and blend well. Turn into a mold lightly coated with mayonnaise.

Flavorful dip made with ingredients right from the refrigerator! Especially good with shrimp.

Spicy Horseradish Dip

1 cup mayonnaise
2 tablespoons prepared horseradish
1 teaspoon cider or white vinegar
½ teaspoon curry powder
½ teaspoon garlic salt
½ teaspoon ground mustard

Combine the mayonnaise, horseradish, vinegar, curry, garlic salt and mustard in a bowl; mix well. Cover and chill for one hour.

Makes 1 cup.

Chicken Nut Spread

10-ounce can chicken breast meat, drained
3½ tablespoons mayonnaise
1 tablespoon lemon juice
2 ounces chopped walnuts
1 teaspoon curry powder

Combine the chicken, mayonnaise, lemon juice, walnuts and curry powder; mix well. Serve on rye bread.

Benedictine Cheese Spread

1 medium cucumber, peeled and seeded
8-ounce package cream cheese, at room temperature
1 small onion, finely-grated
½ teaspoon salt
Dash of Tabasco sauce
Mayonnaise
2 drops green food coloring

A Derby day tradition!

Finely grind the cucumber pulp. Place the pulp in a piece of cheesecloth and press the juice out of the pulp until the pulp is fairly dry. Mash the cream cheese with a fork in a bowl. Add the pulp to the cream cheese and mix thoroughly. Add the onion, salt and Tabasco sauce. Add enough of the mayonnaise to make a smooth, easy-to-spread filling. Add the food coloring to make the filling pale green in color. Combine thoroughly and use for finger sandwiches or as a filling for celery sticks.

Shrimp Ball

8-ounce package cream cheese, at room temperature
6 ounces tiny shrimp
¼ cup minced onion
1 tablespoon horseradish
1 tablespoon mayonnaise
Chopped pecans

Combine the cream cheese, shrimp, onion, horseradish and mayonnaise by hand in a small bowl. Shape the mixture into a ball or log and chill overnight. Roll the ball in the pecans before serving.

Salmon Mousse

10¾-ounce can tomato soup
10¾-ounce can cream of shrimp soup
8 ounces cream cheese
1 cup mayonnaise
3 tablespoons unflavored gelatin
¾ cup water
1 cup pink or red salmon
1¼ cups finely-chopped celery
2 tablespoons chopped onion
Chopped parsley
Cherry tomatoes
Baby shrimp

Combine the tomato soup, cream of shrimp soup, cream cheese and mayonnaise in a saucepan and cook until the mixture is bubbly. Soften the gelatin in the water. Add the gelatin mixture to the soup mixture, stirring well. Cover and chill until slightly thickened. Remove from the refrigerator. Add the salmon, celery and onion; mix well. Turn the mixture into a coated mold. Chill until set. Garnish with the parsley, cherry tomatoes and baby shrimp.

Cranberry Relish

4 cups cranberries
2 unpeeled, seedless oranges
1½ cups pecans
1½ cups sugar

Process the cranberries, oranges and pecans in a food processor. Add the sugar. Pour the relish into jars. Refrigerate for several days before using. You can freeze the relish for several months.

Green Pepper Jelly

6 large green peppers, stem and seeds removed
6 cups sugar
1½ cups white vinegar
6 ounces fruit pectin
1½ teaspoons Tabasco sauce
3 drops green food coloring

Process the green peppers in a food processor until finely ground. Combine the peppers, sugar and vinegar in a large saucepan. Boil for 3 minutes. Remove the saucepan from the heat and let stand for 5 minutes; strain. Add the fruit pectin, Tabasco sauce and food coloring; stir to mix. Spoon the mixture into 4 sterilized, hot 8-ounce jars, leaving a ½-inch edge from top. Cool and cover with aluminum foil and lids. Serve with butter crackers topped with cream cheese.

Green Tomato Relish

12 green tomatoes
2 onions
2 bell peppers
3 jalapeño peppers
1 tablespoon salt
2 to 3 cups vinegar
1½ to 2 cups sugar

Process the tomatoes, onions and peppers in a food processor. Add water as needed when chopping. Add the salt. Allow to set for 2 hours or overnight to blend the flavors. Strain off the water. Put the relish into sterilized jars, packing loosely. Combine the vinegar and sugar in a saucepan and cook over a medium heat until hot and the sugar dissolves. Pour the mixture over the relish until the jars are full. Seal and refrigerate. Relish can be used with dry beans or turnip greens. Keeps well in the refrigerator for several months.

Makes 3 to 4 pints.

Tasty Barbecue Sauce

1 cup vinegar
1 cup sugar
1 cup mustard
1 cup ketchup
1 teaspoon pepper
1 teaspoon celery salt
1½ teaspoons cayenne pepper
1 tablespoon margarine

Combine the vinegar, sugar, mustard, ketchup, pepper, celery salt, cayenne pepper and margarine in a saucepan. Bring the mixture to a boil. Remove the saucepan from the heat and pour the sauce into jars.

Soy Sauce Marinade

½ cup soy sauce
½ cup water
2 tablespoons lemon juice
1 tablespoon brown sugar
2 tablespoons vegetable oil
¼ teaspoon Tabasco sauce
1 clove garlic, crushed
¼ teaspoon freshly-ground pepper

Combine the soy sauce, water, lemon juice, brown sugar, vegetable oil, Tabasco sauce, garlic and pepper. Use for a marinade on beef, pork or chicken.

Wonderful marinade for grilling any type of meat!

Party Trash

12-ounce box rice or wheat Chex cereal
15-ounce box raisins
12-ounce jar roasted peanuts
2 cups pretzel sticks
1 stick margarine
6-ounce package semisweet chocolate chips
1 cup creamy peanut butter
1-pound box powdered sugar

Combine the cereal, raisins, peanuts and pretzels in a large bowl. Combine the margarine and chocolate chips in a separate bowl; melt in the microwave. Add the peanut butter and mix well. Pour the peanut butter mixture over the cereal mixture and mix. Pour the powdered sugar into a large resealable plastic bag. Add the cereal mixture to the bag and shake well. Store the mixture in a large container and serve as a snack.

Tasty snack that's not too sweet. Will disappear fast.

Holiday Fruit Dip

8 ounces lemon yogurt
8-ounce package sour cream
1 teaspoon ginger
1 tablespoon honey
½ teaspoon grated lemon peel
½ teaspoon lemon juice

Combine the yogurt, sour cream, ginger, honey, lemon peel and lemon juice in a bowl; mix well. Cover and chill for 1 to 2 hours. Serve with assorted fresh fruit.

Makes 1¾ cups.

Strawberry-Banana Breakfast Treat

4 cups orange juice
12 tablespoons nonfat milk powder
1 banana, sliced
20 fresh strawberries, hulled
8 ice cubes

Place the orange juice, milk powder, banana and strawberry slices in a food processor. Cover and blend on high speed. Drop in the ice cubes, one at a time, with the machine running. Blend for 10 seconds or until thick and frothy.

Serves 4.

Peach Slush

16-ounce package frozen unsweetened peaches, slightly thawed
12-ounce can peach or apricot nectar
6-ounce can frozen orange juice concentrate, slightly thawed
White wine, peach wine cooler or lemon-lime carbonated beverage, chilled

Combine the undrained peaches, nectar and orange juice concentrate in a blender container. Cover and blend until smooth. Pour the mixture into ice cube trays. Freeze for 3 to 4 hours or until firm. Store in the freezer until serving time. Remove the frozen cubes from the trays. Place the cubes in a large ice bucket or bowl. Let stand for 20 minutes to thaw slightly. Place two or three cubes into each goblet. Add ¾ cup white wine, wine cooler or carbonated beverage; stir gently to make a slush.

Makes 28 cubes or 10 servings.

Lime Cream Cooler

1 quart vanilla ice cream, slightly softened
1 quart lime sherbet, slightly softened
4 cups skim milk
6-ounce can frozen lemonade concentrate, thawed
6-ounce can frozen limeade concentrate, thawed
2 cups water
4 cups ginger ale

Combine the ice cream, sherbet and milk in a large punch bowl. Combine the lemonade concentrate and limeade concentrate and water in a 1-quart pitcher. Pour over the ice cream mixture. Add the ginger ale, stirring until slightly mixed.

Serves 25.

Front Porch Tea

2 cups sugar
¾ cup powdered lemonade mix
½ cup instant tea mix, unsweetened
1 cup white grape juice
1 gallon water

Combine the sugar, lemonade mix, tea, white grape juice and water in a bowl. Pour into a pitcher and chill until ready to serve.

Serves 20.

A refreshing summertime drink.

Mint Juleps

1 cup sugar
1 cup water
1 cup mint leaves
Crushed ice
100 proof Kentucky bourbon
Mint sprigs

Combine the sugar and water in a saucepan and bring the mixture to a boil. Cover and cook, without stirring, for 5 minutes. Remove the saucepan from the heat and allow the mixture to cool. Bruise the mint leaves with the back of a wooden spoon in a bowl. Place the mint leaves in a jar and add the sugar syrup. Cover and chill for 12 to 25 hours. Strain the mixture and discard the mint when ready to use. Fill mint julep cups or glasses with the crushed ice. Add 1 tablespoon of the syrup and 1 ounce of the bourbon to each glass. Stir and garnish with the mint sprigs.

Makes 21 servings.

Kentucky Tea Punch

1½ cups water
4 cups sugar
46-ounce can pineapple juice
32-ounce can orange juice
1 cup lemon juice
64-ounce bottle white cranberry juice
½ gallon weak tea
2-liter ginger ale
Lemon slices
Orange slices

Combine the water and sugar in a saucepan and cook to form a syrup. Remove the saucepan from the heat; cool. Combine the pineapple juice, orange juice, lemon juice, white cranberry juice and tea. Add the syrup and mix well. Chill until ready to serve. Pour the mixture into a punch bowl and add ginger ale when ready to serve. Garnish with the lemon and orange slices.

Cranberry-Zinfandel Punch

64-ounce bottle cranberry juice cocktail, chilled
750-milliliter bottle red zinfandel wine, chilled
⅓ cup bottled sweetened lime juice
1-liter bottle seltzer, chilled
Lime slices

Combine the cranberry juice cocktail, zinfandel and lime juice in a large pitcher or punch bowl. Chill until ready to serve. Stir in the seltzer just before serving. Garnish with the lime slices.

Serves 20.

Strawberry-Lemonade Punch

Two 6-ounce cans frozen pink lemonade concentrate, undiluted
6-ounce can frozen orange juice concentrate, undiluted
10-ounce package frozen sliced strawberries, thawed
3 cups water
28-ounce bottle ginger ale, chilled

Combine the pink lemonade concentrate, orange juice concentrate, strawberries and water in a punch bowl. Chill. Pour the ginger ale into the juice mixture before serving. Stir well.

Makes 2½ quarts.

Chocolate Eggnog

1 quart chilled, prepared eggnog
1½ cups chocolate milk
¾ cup crème de cacao
1½ cups whipping cream
3 tablespoons powdered sugar
Shaved chocolate

Combine the eggnog, chocolate milk and crème de cacao in a pitcher. Cover and chill. Whip the cream to soft peaks and fold in the powdered sugar when ready to serve. Serve in cups topped with the whipped cream mixture and the shaved chocolate or in a punch bowl with the whipped cream mixture folded in and the shaved chocolate sprinkled over the top.

Makes 12 servings.

Hearthside Hot Toddy

An
enjoyable way
to warm up.

1 teaspoon honey
1 lemon slice
3 ounces Kentucky bourbon
4 ounces boiling water
1 cinnamon stick

Combine the honey, lemon slice and bourbon in a large coffee cup. Pour in the boiling water. Stir with the cinnamon stick. Serve immediately.

Breads, Breakfast & Brunch

Breakfast Before a Day at Fancy Farm and Politics

Strawberry Banana Breakfast Treat, page 26

Summertime Zucchini Bread, page 40

Strawberry Bread, page 42

Hash Brown Omelet, page 49

Good Morning Grits, page 49

Fresh Cantaloupe, Melons and Peaches

Sally Lunn

1 stick butter
½ cup sugar
3 large eggs
1 cup milk
2 cups flour
1 tablespoon baking powder
½ teaspoon salt

Cream the butter and sugar in a large bowl until well blended. Beat the eggs in another bowl and add the milk. Combine the flour, baking powder and salt. Add the flour mixture and the milk mixture alternately to the butter mixture, beating after each addition. Pour the batter into a coated tube pan. Bake at 350 degrees for 30 to 40 minutes or until golden brown. Serve hot with butter.

Makes 10 to 12 servings.

Light Corn Bread

1 cup milk
6 tablespoons sugar
2 teaspoons salt
½ cup butter
½ cup warm water
Two .75-ounce packages dry yeast
2 eggs, beaten
3½ cups flour
1¾ cups yellow cornmeal

Combine the milk, sugar, salt and butter; heat until the milk is scalded and the butter is melted. Combine the warm water and yeast; stir until dissolved. Add the milk mixture, eggs, flour and cornmeal; mix well. Spoon the batter into 2 coated loaf pans. Cover and let rise for 1 hour or until the dough has doubled in size. Bake at 375 degrees for 30 minutes.

Makes 2 loaves.

deSha's Fabulous Corn Bread

2 cups self-rising cornmeal
6 eggs
20 ounces cream-style corn
3 cups sour cream
1½ cups salad oil
⅓ cup sugar

Combine the cornmeal, eggs, corn, sour cream, oil and sugar; mix well. Pour the mixture into a coated 10x15-inch baking dish. Bake at 350 degrees for 40 minutes or until a wooden pick inserted comes out clean.

Best cornbread recipe we have ever used. Visit deSha's Restaurant in Lexington, Kentucky.

Parmesan Monkey Bread

Two 12-ounce packages refrigerated biscuits
¾ cup melted butter or margarine
1 cup grated Parmesan cheese

Separate the biscuits. Place the butter and cheese in separate bowls. Dip each of the biscuits into the melted butter and Parmesan cheese. Place the biscuits in a coated tube pan. Pour any remaining butter over the tops of the biscuits. Sprinkle lightly with the remaining cheese. Bake at 350 degrees for 10 to 12 minutes.

Biscuits with Garlic

5 cups biscuit mix
1 cup shredded Cheddar cheese
14½-ounce can chicken broth with roasted garlic

Combine the biscuit mix, cheese and chicken broth in a bowl to form a soft dough. Drop by spoonfuls onto uncoated baking sheets. Bake at 350 degrees for 15 to 20 minutes until browned.

Makes 24 biscuits.

Christmas Morning Angel Biscuits

5 cups self-rising flour
1 teaspoon baking soda
⅓ cup sugar
1 cup shortening
Two .75-ounce packages dry yeast
¼ cup warm water
2 cups buttermilk

Combine the flour, baking soda and sugar in a bowl. Cut in the shortening. Combine the yeast and water in a cup; mix well. Add the buttermilk and yeast mixture; mix well. Roll the dough on a floured surface. Cut the dough into biscuits. Place the biscuits on a baking sheet and freeze. Place the frozen biscuits in a resealable plastic bag. Bake the frozen biscuits at 400 degrees for 10 to 15 minutes.

Parker House Rolls

.75-ounce package dry yeast
¼ cup warm water
1 cup scalded milk
2 tablespoons shortening
2 tablespoons sugar
1 teaspoon salt
1 egg
3½ cups flour

Dissolve the yeast in the water. Add the milk, shortening, sugar and salt; cool. Add the egg and flour. Let the dough rise in a warm place for 1 to 2 hours or until the dough is double in size. Punch the dough down and form into buns. Allow the buns to rise until light. Bake at 425 degrees until the buns are golden brown.

Mayonnaise Rolls

1 cup self-rising flour
½ cup milk
2 tablespoons mayonnaise

Combine the flour, milk and mayonnaise in a bowl; mix well. Fill coated muffin cups ⅔ full. Bake at 375 degrees for 14 minutes.

Makes 6 rolls.

Old yet easy recipe! Great for new cooks.

Whole Wheat Rolls

1 cup powdered milk
1½ cups brown sugar
1½ teaspoons salt
3 tablespoons dry yeast
2 cups hot water
¼ cup molasses
¼ cup honey
¼ cup butter
1 egg, beaten
2 cups flour
4 cups whole-wheat flour
Melted butter

Combine the milk, brown sugar, salt, yeast, water, molasses, honey and butter in a large bowl. Add the egg to the mixture. Beat in the flour. Beat in the whole-wheat flour, ½ cup at a time, until the mixture is firm but sticky. Add more of the flour if the dough is too sticky. Knead the dough for 10 minutes. Turn the dough into a coated bowl and coat on all sides. Cover the bowl with plastic wrap and set aside for 1 hour or until the dough doubles. Form the dough into balls smaller than the size of a golf ball. Place the balls on a coated baking sheet and brush each ball with the melted butter. Bake at 350 degrees for 20 to 25 minutes.

Makes 3 dozen rolls.

Bread for Bread Machine

Two cup loaf

1½ teaspoons yeast
2 cups bread flour
1 teaspoon salt
2 teaspoons sugar
1½ tablespoons powdered milk
½ cup plus 1 tablespoon butter
½ cup water
1 egg

Combine the yeast, flour, salt, sugar, milk, butter, water and egg in a bowl. Place in the bread machine and cook according to the manufacturer's directions.

Three cup loaf

1¾ teaspoons yeast
3 cups bread flour
1½ teaspoons salt
1 tablespoon sugar
2½ tablespoons powdered milk
½ cup plus 2 tablespoons butter
⅔ cup water
2 eggs

Combine the yeast, flour, salt, sugar, milk, butter, water and eggs in a bowl. Place in the bread machine and cook according to the manufacturer's directions.

A good idea is to freeze the zucchini during the summer when it is plentiful. Just shred and place it in a resealable bag.

Summertime Zucchini Bread

3 cups flour
1 cup chopped walnuts
2 teaspoons baking soda
1½ teaspoons ground cinnamon
1 teaspoon salt
1 teaspoon ground nutmeg
½ teaspoon baking powder
3 large eggs
1 cup light olive oil
2 cups sugar
2 teaspoons vanilla extract
2 cups unpeeled shredded zucchini
8¼-ounce can crushed pineapple, drained

Combine the flour, walnuts, baking soda, cinnamon, salt, nutmeg and baking powder in a medium bowl. Beat the eggs in a large bowl with an electric mixer on high speed. Beat in the oil, sugar and vanilla extract until the mixture is thick and foamy. Stir in the zucchini, pineapple and flour mixture. Pour the mixture into 2 coated 4x8-inch loaf pans. Bake at 350 degrees for 1 hour. Allow the bread to cool for 10 minutes and turn out onto wire racks.

Cinnamon Raisin Bread

1½ cups milk
½ cup margarine
2 teaspoons salt
½ cup sugar
1 cup unseasoned mashed potatoes
Two .75-ounce packages dry yeast
½ cup warm water
7½ cups flour
1½ cups raisins
½ cup sugar
2 teaspoons cinnamon
Melted butter

Heat the milk in a saucepan until bubbles form around the edges. Remove the saucepan from the heat and add the margarine, salt, sugar and potatoes; mix well. Allow the mixture to cool. Sprinkle the yeast in the water. Combine the yeast and milk mixture in a bowl and mix well. Combine the flour and raisins in a separate bowl. Add the raisin mixture to the dough. Turn the dough onto a floured board and knead for 8 to 10 minutes. Place the dough in a coated bowl and allow to rise until doubled. Punch the dough down and divide in half. Roll each half into a 8x16-inch rectangle. Combine the sugar and cinnamon and sprinkle onto each rectangle. Roll each rectangle into a jelly roll and place in two loaf pans. Brush the tops with the melted butter. Allow the dough to set in a warm place to rise. Brush again with the melted butter. Bake at 375 degrees for 30 to 35 minutes.

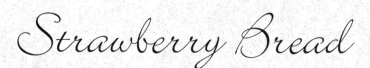

Strawberry Bread

3 cups self-rising flour
2 cups sugar
3 eggs, beaten
1½ cups oil
2 teaspoons cinnamon
2½ cups strawberries
1 teaspoon vanilla extract
1 cup chopped pecans

Combine the flour, sugar, eggs, oil, cinnamon, strawberries, vanilla extract and pecans in a large bowl; mix well. Pour the batter into two coated and floured loaf pans. Bake at 350 degrees for 60 minutes.

Serves 24.

Village Hush Puppies

1 cup self-rising cornmeal
½ cup self-rising flour
1 teaspoon salt
¼ teaspoon garlic powder
2 tablespoons chopped, dried chives
¼ teaspoon paprika
¼ cup minced onion
¾ cup buttermilk

Combine the cornmeal, flour, salt, garlic powder, chives, paprika and onion in a bowl. Add the buttermilk and mix well. Shape the mixture with a small ice cream scoop or a teaspoon. Drop the balls into a deep fryer heated to 300 degrees. Cook for 5 minutes or until golden brown.

Makes 12 to 16 hushpuppies.

For years Kentucky Dam Village has served these delicious hush puppies.

Six Weeks Bran Muffins

15-ounce box Raisin Bran cereal
5 cups flour
3 cups sugar
5 teaspoons baking soda
2 teaspoons salt
4 eggs
1 quart buttermilk

Combine the cereal, flour, sugar, baking soda, salt, eggs and buttermilk in a large bowl; mix well. Store in the refrigerator in an airtight container for up to six weeks. Spoon out as needed. Pour the batter into coated muffin cups. Bake at 400 degrees for 15 minutes.

Add ½ teaspoon of your favorite jam to each muffin cup before baking for a nice surprise.

Best Ever No-Fat Muffins

1½ cups self-rising flour
¾ cup light brown sugar
½ cup peeled, grated apple
2 teaspoons ground cinnamon
⅔ cup skim milk
⅔ cup plain low-fat yogurt

Combine the flour, sugar, apple and cinnamon in a large mixing bowl. Stir in the milk and yogurt, just until mixed. Pour the mixture into 12 lightly-coated muffin cups. Bake at 400 degrees for 15 minutes.

This recipe has been around for years but it is a "must" for everyone. Makes a big tubful!

Try this— it's healthy and uses no eggs or oil.

Breakfast Pizza

One 8-ounce can refrigerated crescent rolls
6 eggs, beaten
½ pound bacon, cooked and crumbled
1 cup shredded Cheddar cheese
½ cup sliced fresh mushrooms

Spread the rolls onto a coated 12-inch baking sheet, pressing firmly to seal the perforations. Bake at 375 degrees for 2 minutes. Combine the eggs, bacon, cheese and mushrooms; pour over the crust. Bake at 375 degrees for 12 to 15 minutes.

Overnight Deluxe French Toast

8 slices French bread
4 eggs
1 cup milk
1 tablespoon sugar
⅛ teaspoon salt
2 tablespoons orange juice
½ teaspoon vanilla extract
2 tablespoons butter
Powdered sugar

Place the bread slices into a 9x13-inch baking dish. Combine the eggs, milk, sugar, salt, orange juice and vanilla extract; mix well. Pour the egg mixture over the bread slices and turn the bread to coat. Cover the baking dish and chill overnight. Melt the butter in a large skillet. Sauté the bread for 4 minutes on each side or until brown. Sprinkle with the powdered sugar and serve.

Breakfast Hash Browns

3 medium potatoes, cooked and cooled
¼ teaspoon salt
⅛ teaspoon black pepper
½ cup shredded reduced-fat sharp Cheddar cheese
2 slices turkey bacon, cooked and crumbled
2 green onions, finely chopped

Peel and grate the potatoes. Season the potatoes with the salt and pepper. Place ½ of the potatoes in an even layer in a coated skillet. Cover the potatoes with the cheese, bacon and green onions; add the remaining potatoes. Cook over a high heat for 5 minutes, shaking the skillet gently to keep the potato cake loose. Lift the edges with a spatula to see when the potatoes have a golden brown crust. Place a plate over the skillet and invert the potatoes onto the plate. Slide the potatoes back into the coated skillet, uncooked side down. Cook for 5 minutes longer or until the potatoes are golden brown. Cut the potato cake into wedges and serve immediately.

Serves 4.

Waffles

2 cups biscuit mix
½ cup vegetable oil
2 eggs
1 cup club soda

Combine the biscuit mix, oil and eggs in a large bowl. Add the club soda, stirring until well blended. Cook in a preheated waffle iron until the waffles are golden.

Makes ten 4-inch waffles.

Light and airy version of waffles.

Granola is so nice to have on hand. Pour a cup in a cookie recipe, over cereal, in a dish of yogurt— be creative.

Granola

4 cups oatmeal
1½ cups wheat germ
1 cup grated coconut
¼ cup powdered milk
1 to 2 tablespoons cinnamon
1 tablespoon brown sugar
⅓ cup vegetable oil
½ cup honey
1 tablespoon vanilla extract
½ cup sesame seeds
½ cup nuts or raisins

Combine the oatmeal, wheat germ, coconut, milk, cinnamon and brown sugar in a bowl. Combine the oil, honey and vanilla extract in a saucepan and heat. Add the oil mixture to the oatmeal mixture and stir until blended. Spread the mixture on coated baking sheets. Bake at 250 degrees for 1 hour, turning with a spatula occasionally. Add the sesame seeds, nuts or raisins when toasted. Allow to cool and store in an airtight container.

Strawberry Sour Cream Coffee Cake

1 egg, lightly beaten
8 ounces sour cream
½ cup milk
Two 7-ounce packages strawberry muffin mix
½ cup powdered sugar
1 tablespoon milk
¼ teaspoon vanilla extract

Combine the egg, sour cream, milk and muffin mix; mix well. Pour the mixture into a coated round 9-inch cake pan. Bake at 350 degrees for 35 to 40 minutes. Cool the coffee cake for 10 minutes and remove from the pan. Combine the powdered sugar, milk and vanilla extract and mix well. Drizzle the mixture over the cake.

Apple Fritters

1 cup flour
1½ teaspoons baking powder
½ teaspoon salt
2 tablespoons sugar
1 egg
½ cup plus 1 tablespoon milk
1½ cups peeled, diced apples

Sift the flour, baking powder, salt and sugar in a large bowl. Beat the egg and add the milk. Pour the egg mixture into the flour mixture. Stir until the batter is smooth. Add the apples to the batter and mix well. Drop the batter by spoonfuls into deep hot oil. Fry until golden brown.

Makes 12 to 15 fritters.

Fruit Coffee Cake Squares

1 cup fat-free sour cream
¼ cup water
3 egg whites
18¼-ounce package super-moist light white cake mix
10-ounce jar low-sugar fruit spread or 21-ounce can fruit pie filling
Powdered sugar

Combine the sour cream, water and egg whites in a large bowl. Add the cake mix and stir until moistened; the batter will be lumpy. Spread the mixture onto a coated baking pan. Drop the fruit spread by rounded spoonfuls onto the batter; swirl the spread on top of the batter, using the back of a spoon. Bake at 350 degrees for 25 to 30 minutes or until the cake springs back when touched; cool. Sprinkle with the powdered sugar.

Serves 16.

Good Morning Grits

8 cups half-and-half
1 teaspoon salt
½ teaspoon garlic powder
½ teaspoon pepper
2 cups quick-cooking grits
8-ounce package cream cheese, cubed
12-ounce package shredded Cheddar cheese
1 teaspoon Tabasco sauce

Combine the half-and-half, salt, garlic powder and pepper in a saucepan and bring to a boil. Stir in the grits and return to a boil; cover and reduce the heat. Simmer for 5 minutes, stirring occasionally. Add the cream cheese, Cheddar cheese and Tabasco sauce. Stir the mixture until the cheese is melted.

Serves 8 to 12.

Hash Brown Omelet

6 medium potatoes
12 eggs
3 cups diced, cooked ham
1 cup diced green pepper
3 cups shredded Cheddar cheese
Parsley
Orange slices

Peel and shred the potatoes. Place the potatoes in a medium-hot skillet in single serving portions, about 2 cups each. Spread the potatoes while cooking to crisp. Scramble the eggs, diced ham and green pepper in a separate skillet. Place 1½ cups of the egg mixture on top of each of the potato servings. Cover each serving with ½ cup of the Cheddar cheese. Fold the potatoes, turn once, and cook for 3 minutes. Place the omelets on plates and garnish with the parsley and orange slices.

Makes 6 servings.

Asparagus-Mushroom Omelet

Nothing beats fresh asparagus in the spring in Kentucky.

1 large egg
5 large egg whites
1 tablespoon minced fresh chives
2 tablespoons cold water
¼ teaspoon black pepper
2 tablespoons low-fat margarine
¼ cup finely-chopped cooked asparagus or broccoli
¼ cup finely-chopped mushrooms
¼ cup finely-chopped tomato
¼ cup minced parsley

Combine the egg, egg whites, chives, water and pepper in a bowl; whisk to lightly mix. Melt ½ tablespoon of the margarine in a heavy skillet over a moderately-high heat. Add ¼ each of the asparagus or broccoli and mushroom and cook for 1 minute, stirring constantly. Add ½ cup of the egg mixture; cook until the bottom is set. Fold the omelet in half or roll it to the edge of the pan and invert it onto a heated plate. Make 3 more omelets in the same way. Top each omelet with the chopped tomato and sprinkle with the parsley.

- Serves 4.

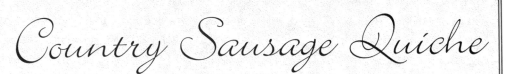

Country Sausage Quiche

12 ounces bulk sausage
½ cup chopped onion
Two 9-inch unbaked piecrusts
8 ounces shredded mozzarella cheese
8 eggs, beaten
1½ cups milk
1 teaspoon salt
½ teaspoon pepper

Brown the sausage and onion in a skillet; drain. Divide the sausage mixture evenly between the 2 piecrusts. Combine the cheese, eggs, milk, salt and pepper. Pour the egg mixture evenly over the sausage in each quiche. Bake at 375 degrees for 30 minutes.

Serves 16.

Spring Asparagus Quiche

1 pound fresh asparagus
½ cup chopped onion
4 large mushrooms, sliced
2 tablespoons margarine
6 eggs, beaten
1 cup shredded four cheese blend
2 cups half-and-half
Salt and pepper to taste
9-inch pie crust

Wash the asparagus and cut 1 inch off of the stems. Cut the asparagus into 1 inch pieces. Sauté the asparagus, onion and mushrooms in the margarine in a large skillet until the onion is transparent. Combine the eggs, cheese, half-and-half and salt and pepper; mix well. Add the asparagus mixture and stir. Pour the mixture into the piecrust and bake at 350 degrees for 35 minutes or until golden brown.

Brunch Torte

1 cup shredded Cheddar cheese
Two 9-inch unbaked piecrusts
¾ pound thinly-sliced cooked ham
1½ cups thinly-sliced, unpeeled red potatoes
1 medium onion, sliced
10-ounce package frozen spinach, thawed and drained
1 egg
1 tablespoon water

Sprinkle ⅓ cup of the cheese on one of the crusts. Place ½ of the ham, potatoes and onion on top of the cheese. Place the spinach evenly on the top. Cover the spinach with ⅓ cup of the cheese and the remaining ham, potatoes and onion. Sprinkle the remaining cheese on top and gently press the mixture into the piecrust. Top with the remaining piecrust, folding the top crust over the edges and pinching to seal. Cut slits in the top piecrust. Combine the egg and water in a cup and brush the top with the mixture. Place the torte on a baking sheet and bake at 375 degrees for 45 to 60 minutes or until the crust is golden brown.

Serves 8.

Breakfast or brunch, guests will love this version with potatoes.

Simple Salsa Egg Bake

12 eggs
½ cup half-and-half
11-ounce can whole kernel corn with red and green peppers
Ten 6-inch corn tortillas, cut into squares
4 ounces shredded Cheddar cheese
2 cups salsa
1 cup sour cream
1 cup guacamole

Combine the eggs and half-and-half in a bowl and beat slightly; add the corn. Place the tortilla squares in the bottom of a coated 9x13-inch baking dish. Pour the egg mixture over the squares. Sprinkle the egg mixture with the cheese. Cover and chill overnight.

Cover and bake at 375 degrees for 25 to 30 minutes or until the eggs are set. Let stand, covered, for 5 minutes. Uncover and top with the salsa. Serve with the sour cream and guacamole.

Serves 12 to 15.

Fast Break Sausage and Egg Casserole

1½ pounds sausage
9 eggs, lightly beaten
3 cups milk
1½ teaspoons dry mustard
1 teaspoon salt
3 slices white bread, cut into ⅛-inch cubes
1½ cups grated Cheddar cheese

Brown the sausage and drain. Spread the sausage into a 9x13-inch baking dish. Combine the eggs, milk, mustard, salt, bread cubes and cheese in a mixing bowl; mix well. Spread the mixture over the sausage. Cover and chill overnight. Uncover and bake at 350 degrees for 1 hour. Cut into squares before serving.

Serves 8.

Soups, Salads & Sandwiches

Picnic by the Lake

Derby Afternoon Cheese Straws, page 17

Dockside Crab Dip, page 18

Turkey Brew Burgers, page 81

Combined Pasta Salad, page 66

Dried Apple Pies, page 166

Speedy Little Devils, page 160

Soft Drinks and Coffee

Dinner Party Artichoke Soup

1 small onion, finely chopped
4 tablespoons butter
2 tablespoons flour
½ cup milk
14-ounce can artichokes, drained and chopped, reserving liquid
3 cups chicken consommé or broth
3 egg yolks
½ cup cream
1 teaspoon lemon juice
Salt to taste
Sour cream
Lemon slices

Sauté the onion in the butter in a saucepan. Blend in the flour and milk, stirring until well blended. Add the artichoke liquid and chicken consommé; bring to a boil. Combine the egg yolks and cream. Remove 1 cup of the hot liquid and add to the egg yolk mixture; stir well and return to the saucepan. Add the chopped artichokes, lemon juice and salt. Garnish with a spoonful of the sour cream and a lemon slice.

Serves 6 to 8.

Baked Potato and Corn Soup

4 large baking potatoes
1 stick butter
⅔ cup flour
6 cups milk
2 cups fresh corn
Salt and white pepper to taste
¾ cup finely-chopped onion
10 slices bacon, cooked and crumbled, divided
1¼ cups shredded sharp Cheddar cheese, divided
8-ounce package sour cream
Snipped fresh chives

Pierce each potato a few times with the tines of a fork. Bake the potatoes at 400 degrees for 1 hour or until cooked through. Allow the potatoes to cool completely and cut them in half lengthwise and scoop out the pulp. Melt the butter in a heavy saucepan over a medium heat. Add the flour, stirring to make a smooth, lump-free mixture. Cook for 1 minute, stirring constantly. Slowly add the milk, cooking over a medium heat, stirring constantly, until the mixture begins to thicken. Add the potato pulp, corn, salt, pepper, onion, ½ of the crumbled bacon and ¾ cup of the cheese. Cook until heated through. Add the sour cream and stir. Add more milk for a soup that's not so thick. Serve the soup at once, sprinkling the remaining bacon and cheese on top. Add a sprinkle of the chives if desired.

Serves 8 to 10.

If ham is used, sauté the ham and onion in bacon grease.

Creamy Clam Chowder

½ cup chopped raw bacon or diced ham
½ onion, diced
Butter
2 potatoes, chopped
Two 6½-ounce cans minced clams, undrained
Milk or half-and-half
2 to 3 tablespoons butter
Instant mashed potatoes
Salt and pepper to taste

Sauté the bacon and onion in a small amount of the butter in a skillet until the onion is transparent. Add the potatoes, clams and enough water to cover. Cook until the potatoes are tender. Add enough of the milk or half-and-half to make 1 quart. Add the 2 to 3 tablespoons butter. Add the instant mashed potatoes, ½ tablespoon at a time, until the chowder is the desired thickness. Season with the salt and pepper.

Serves 4 to 5.

Cabbage and Bison Soup

1 pound ground bison
16-ounce can kidney beans, undrained
28-ounce can tomatoes, chopped
1 tomato can of water
½ head cabbage, chopped
2 celery stalks, chopped
4 beef bouillon cubes
½ teaspoon garlic salt
¼ teaspoon garlic powder
¼ teaspoon black pepper

Brown the bison in a Dutch oven; drain. Add the beans, tomatoes, water, cabbage, celery, bouillon cubes, garlic salt, garlic power and pepper. Bring the mixture to a boil. Reduce the heat and simmer, covered, for 1 hour.

Red Onion Soup

5 cups thinly-sliced red onions
3 tablespoons butter
3 tablespoons flour
½ cup Kentucky bourbon
2 quarts beef broth
¼ teaspoon basil
8 slices French bread, toasted
8 slices Swiss cheese

Sauté the onions in the butter in a saucepan until the onions are transparent. Stir in the flour using a fork, making a paste. Pour in the bourbon and broth; season with the basil. Reduce the heat and simmer for 30 minutes. Place one slice of bread per serving in the bottom of an ovenproof bowl. Ladle the onion soup, approximately ¾ cup, onto the bread. Cover with a cheese slice. Broil on low until the cheese is bubbly. Serve while hot.

Serves 8.

A rich soup to warm the soul and share with friends.

Healthy & Easy White Bean Soup

1½ cups dry northern beans
5 cups water
2 boneless, skinless chicken breasts
1.25-ounce envelope taco seasoning mix
Salt and pepper to taste
2 cups picante sauce

Wash the beans and place in a slow cooker. Add the water, chicken and ½ of the taco seasoning. Season with the salt and pepper. Pour the picante sauce on top. Place the lid on the cooker and set on high. Cook for 7 hours, checking to see if more water is needed about midway. Tear the chicken using a fork and stir before serving.

Serves 4.

Cream of Vegetable Soup

2 tablespoons butter
1 clove garlic, chopped
1 medium onion, sliced
¼ head cauliflower, broken
2 carrots, chopped
2 stalks celery, chopped
6 asparagus stalks, chopped
1 leek, chopped
1 large potato, peeled and chopped
1 cup chopped spinach
Salt and pepper to taste
1 quart chicken broth
Pinch of cayenne pepper
1 cup heavy cream

The best and most unusual vegetable soup you'll have ever eaten!

3 tablespoons flour
1 tablespoon chopped parsley
1 tablespoon Parmesan cheese

Melt the butter in a stockpot. Add the garlic and onion and sauté for 3 minutes. Add the cauliflower, carrots, celery, asparagus, leek, potato and spinach. Season with the salt and pepper; cook for 5 to 6 minutes. Add the chicken broth and cayenne pepper and simmer for 25 to 30 minutes. Combine the cream and flour in a cup until smooth. Pour the mixture slowly into the soup, stirring constantly. Simmer until the soup begins to thicken. Serve the soup topped with the parsley and Parmesan cheese.

Cumberland House Cream of Mushroom Soup

2 cups sliced, fresh mushrooms
½ cup finely-chopped onion
2 tablespoons butter or margarine
2 cups chicken broth or 10¾-ounce can cream of chicken soup
2 tablespoons all-purpose flour
¼ teaspoon salt
¼ teaspoon white pepper
1½ cups milk

Sauté the mushrooms and onion in the butter in a stockpot until the mushrooms are tender. Add the broth or soup, flour, salt and white pepper. Reduce the heat and slowly add the milk. Stir often until steam appears, without boiling. Serve immediately.

Serves 4 to 6.

The best of the best of mushroom soups. Served at the Cumberland House Restaurant in Kuttawa, Kentucky.

Loaded Potato Soup

2 cups coarsely-chopped celery
2 cups coarsely-chopped onion
2 cups sliced carrots
¾ teaspoon white pepper
Two 14-ounce cans chicken broth
2 broth cans water
3 cups diced potatoes
1 cup whipping cream
½ cup flour
2 tablespoons butter
Bacon bits
Green onions, sliced
Sour cream

Combine the celery, onion, carrots, pepper, chicken broth and water in a saucepan. Bring the mixture to a boil and boil until the vegetables are tender. Add the potatoes and cream. Simmer for 15 to 20 minutes. Blend the flour and butter; add the mixture to the soup. Simmer until thickened. Season to taste. Serve topped with the bacon bits, green onions and sour cream.

Serves 10 to 12.

Pasta Salad

12-ounce package roasted garlic and red pepper fettuccini
4 to 8 ounces feta cheese, crumbled
½ sweet onion, finely chopped
3 cups quartered cherry tomatoes or halved grape tomatoes
10 fresh basil leaves, sliced into thin strips

Balsamic Vinaigrette

¼ cup balsamic vinegar
1 heaping teaspoon Dijon mustard
2 cloves garlic, minced
¾ cup olive oil

Break the pasta into bite-size pieces and cook according to the package directions until tender. Drain the pasta, rinse in cold water and drain again. Combine the pasta, cheese, onion, tomatoes and basil in a bowl. Combine the vinegar, mustard and garlic in a blender container. Add the olive oil in a fine stream, while blending at a high speed, until the mixture is smooth. Add the vinaigrette as desired to the salad; stir gently. Serve the salad warm.

Makes 6 servings.

Asparagus Pasta Salad

1 cup small shell pasta, cooked
1½ cups cut asparagus
½ cup thinly-sliced carrots
½ cup diced onion
¼ cup diced red pepper
½ to ¾ cup Zesty low-fat Italian salad dressing
1 teaspoon oregano
½ teaspoon celery seed

Cook the pasta according to the package directions. Rinse, drain and allow to cool. Add the asparagus, carrots, onion, pepper, dressing, oregano and celery seed; mix well. Chill and marinate for 6 to 8 hours or overnight. Serve cold.

Serves 4.

Great accompaniment to grilled burgers and serves a crowd!

Combined Pasta Salad

2 cups broccoli florets
1 onion, separated into rings
1 green pepper, coarsely chopped
Two 6-ounce jars artichoke hearts, drained and rinsed
6 green onions, sliced
½ cup fat-free Ranch dressing
¼ cup picante sauce
1 head lettuce, torn into bite-size pieces
8 black olives, sliced
½ cup shredded mozzarella cheese
2 tomatoes, diced
1 cup small shell pasta, cooked and drained
2 tablespoons oregano
Salt and pepper to taste

Combine the broccoli, onion, pepper, artichokes and green onions in a medium bowl. Combine the dressing and picante sauce; pour over the vegetables. Cover and chill for 3 hours. Add the lettuce, black olives, cheese, tomatoes, pasta, oregano, salt and pepper. Toss well and serve.

Serves 12.

Party Fleur-de-lis

1 head red leaf lettuce
36 jumbo shrimp, cooked and deveined
6 avocados, cut into wedges
2 grapefruit, sectioned
11-ounce can mandarin orange sections, drained
12 cherry tomatoes

Arrange the lettuce leaves on salad plates. Arrange the shrimp, avocado wedges, grapefruit sections, mandarin oranges and tomatoes on the lettuce. Serve with Remoulade Sauce.

Remoulade Sauce

1 bunch green onions, chopped
¼ cup finely-chopped celery
1 clove garlic, chopped
¼ cup parsley
⅓ cup white vinegar
3 tablespoons hot Creole mustard
1 tablespoon paprika
½ teaspoon salt
¼ teaspoon pepper
⅔ cup olive oil

Combine the onions, celery, garlic and parsley in a food processor and pulse until chopped. Add the vinegar, mustard, paprika, salt and pepper. Add the olive oil in a slow steady stream while the processor is running. Serve over Party Fleur-de-lis.

Serves 12 as a salad or 6 as the main course.

Mixed Vegetable Salad

¾ cup white vinegar
½ cup vegetable oil
1 cup sugar
1 teaspoon salt
1 teaspoon pepper
15¼-ounce can whole kernel corn, drained
15-ounce can peas, drained
14½-ounce can green beans, drained
1 cup diced bell pepper
1 cup diced celery
1 cup chopped onion
1 cup shredded carrots

Combine the vinegar, oil, sugar, salt and pepper in a saucepan. Bring the mixture to a boil, stirring until the sugar dissolves; cool. Combine the corn, peas, green beans, pepper, celery, onion and carrots in a bowl. Pour the vinegar mixture over the vegetables and chill for 8 hours or overnight.

Any vegetable may be substituted and can size is a matter of preference.

Shrimp Rice Curry Salad

1 cup cooked rice
4-ounce can shrimp
1 cup diced celery
3 tablespoons finely-chopped onion
¾ teaspoon curry powder
1 tablespoon vinegar
2 tablespoons salad oil
¼ green pepper, finely chopped
¾ cup mayonnaise

Combine the rice, shrimp, celery and onion. Add the curry powder, vinegar, oil, pepper and mayonnaise; mix well.

Sauerkraut Salad

1 cup sugar
½ cup white vinegar
27-ounce can sauerkraut, drained
2-ounce jar pimento
½ cup chopped green onion
½ cup chopped green pepper
1 tablespoon mustard seed
1 tablespoon celery seed
½ cup vegetable oil

Combine the sugar and vinegar in a saucepan; bring the mixture to a boil. Set the mixture aside to cool. Combine the sauerkraut, pimento, onion, pepper, mustard seed and celery seed in a large bowl. Pour the vegetable oil over the vegetable mixture. Pour the cooled vinegar mixture over the vegetable mixture. Marinate, chilled, for 24 hours.

Red Green Slaw

3 cups shredded green cabbage
3 cups shredded red cabbage
1 green pepper, finely chopped
1 large onion, finely chopped
1 teaspoon celery seed
1 teaspoon salt
¼ teaspoon ground black pepper
2 tablespoons sugar
½ cup mayonnaise
½ teaspoon paprika
1 teaspoon prepared mustard
2 tablespoons lemon juice

Combine the red cabbage, green cabbage, green pepper and onion; toss. Add the celery seed, salt, pepper and sugar; mix well. Combine the mayonnaise, paprika, mustard and lemon juice and mix well. Pour the mayonnaise mixture over the vegetable mixture and mix thoroughly. This salad is best when the vegetables and dressing are prepared ahead and chilled until just before they are mixed for the table.

Chutney can be made with equal parts of sweet pickle relish and jam or marmalade.

Curried Broccoli Salad

2 bunches broccoli
2 to 2½ cups red grapes, cut in half
½ red onion, sliced
½ cup slivered almonds, toasted
1 cup mayonnaise
9 ounces chutney
2 teaspoons curry powder

Cut the broccoli into florets discarding the stems. Dice the broccoli. Combine the broccoli, grapes, onion and almonds in a bowl. Combine the mayonnaise, chutney and curry powder in a separate bowl; mixing well. Combine the broccoli mixture and the dressing mixture and blend well. Chill for 1 hour before serving to allow the flavors to blend.

Serves 6 to 8.

Taffy Apple Salad

20-ounce can pineapple chunks, drained, reserving juice
2 cups miniature marshmallows
½ cup brown sugar
1 tablespoon flour
1 egg, well beaten
1½ tablespoons vinegar
12-ounce container whipped topping
2 cups diced apples, unpeeled
1½ cups Spanish peanuts

Combine the pineapple and marshmallows in a bowl. Chill overnight. Combine the pineapple juice, brown sugar, flour, egg and vinegar in a saucepan. Cook over a medium heat until thick. Chill overnight. Combine the sauce and the whipped topping; mix well. Add the pineapple mixture, apples and peanuts. Chill for 8 hours before serving.

A tasty alternative to the original apple salad. Especially nice fall dish.

Fruit Salad with Honey Dressing

1 cup grapefruit sections
1 cup sliced bananas
1 cup sliced peaches, drained
1 cup orange sections
1 cup pineapple chunks
1 cup chopped pecans
8-ounce package cream cheese, at room temperature
¼ cup honey
Juice of 1 lemon
1 cup whipping cream
Mint leaves

Combine the grapefruit, bananas, peaches, orange and pineapple in a bowl. Add the pecans and chill. Blend the cream cheese, honey and lemon juice until smooth. Whip the cream until soft peaks form. Fold the cream into the cream cheese mixture. Pour the mixture over the fruit. Garnish with the mint leaves.

Slimming Seafood Salad

2 pounds imitation crab meat
2 stalks celery, coarsely chopped
8 tablespoons fat-free mayonnaise
1 teaspoon salt
½ teaspoon pepper
4 cups coarsely-chopped lettuce
2 teaspoons paprika
4 scallions, chopped

Combine the crab meat, celery, mayonnaise, salt and pepper in a bowl. Place the lettuce on a serving platter and top with the crab meat mixture. Sprinkle with the paprika and scallions.

Serves 4.

Beautiful presentation & the balsamic dressing can be used with other salads. A good, basic and easy salad.

Orange Almond Salad

1 head Bibb or Romaine lettuce, washed and torn
1 red onion, sliced into rings
Mandarin oranges, strawberries or fruit of your choice
2 tablespoons sugar
½ cup olive oil
3 tablespoons balsamic vinegar
1 teaspoon lemon juice
½ teaspoon salt
½ teaspoon dry mustard
½ teaspoon minced onion
Slivered, toasted almonds

Place the lettuce in a large bowl and top with the onion rings and fruit. Combine the sugar, olive oil, vinegar, lemon juice, salt, mustard and onion in a separate bowl and whisk. Pour the dressing over the salad and top with the almonds.

Serves 6.

Fancy Rice Salad

2 cups cooked brown rice, cooled
1 cup diced celery
1 cup shredded carrots
1 large apple, peeled and diced
1 large green or red pepper, cut into narrow strips
1 red onion, cut into strips
½ cup toasted pecans
½ cup Italian dressing
1 teaspoon Dijon mustard
1 to 2 tablespoons sugar

Combine the rice, celery, carrots, apple, pepper, onion and pecans in a large bowl. Add the dressing, mustard and sugar; mix well. Cover and chill until ready to serve.

Serves 4.

Marinated Veggie Salad

16-ounce can green peas, drained
16-ounce can French-style green beans, drained
2-ounce jar chopped pimento
4 celery stalks, chopped
1 medium red onion, chopped
½ cup salad oil
1 cup red wine vinegar
1 tablespoon salt
1 cup sugar
1 teaspoon paprika

Combine the peas, green beans, pimento, celery and onion in a large bowl. Combine the oil, vinegar, salt, sugar and paprika in a small bowl. Pour the dressing over the vegetables. Chill for 24 hours. Drain and serve.

Rice and Artichoke Salad

6.9-ounce package chicken flavored Rice-A-Roni
Two 6-ounce jars marinated artichokes, drained and chopped,
reserving the liquid
2 green onions, sliced
½ green pepper, chopped
8 olives, sliced
¼ teaspoon curry
½ cup mayonnaise
3 cooked chicken breasts, chopped

Cook the rice according to the package directions, omitting the butter. Cool the rice to room temperature and add the artichokes. Combine the onions, pepper, olives and reserved artichoke liquid. Add the curry and mayonnaise and mix well. Add the mixture to the rice and mix well. Allow the rice to stand for several hours. Add the chicken when ready to serve.

Serves 7.

French Dressing

2 cups sugar
1 grated onion
1 pint cooking oil
4 teaspoons paprika
1 cup vinegar
24-ounce bottle ketchup
4 teaspoons salt
Juice of 2 lemons

Combine the sugar, onion, oil, paprika, vinegar, ketchup, salt and lemon juice in a bowl. Whisk until the mixture is well mixed. Pour the dressing into a bottle and store in the refrigerator.

Thousand Island Dressing

1 cup mayonnaise
½ teaspoon grated onion
2 tablespoons finely-chopped green pepper
½ teaspoon finely-chopped chives
6 tablespoons chili sauce
⅛ teaspoon chili powder

Combine the mayonnaise, onion, pepper, chives, chili sauce and chili powder in a bowl; mix well. Pour the dressing into a bottle and store in the refrigerator.

Simple Salsa Dressing

1 cup mayonnaise
¼ cup salsa
⅛ cup chopped cilantro, optional

Combine the mayonnaise and salsa in a small bowl and mix well. Add the cilantro and stir. Store in the refrigerator in an airtight container.

This mixture is so good and easy to make.

Veggie Burgers

2 eggs
⅓ cup plain yogurt
2 teaspoons Worcestershire sauce
2 teaspoons curry powder
½ teaspoon salt
¼ teaspoon ground red pepper
1⅓ cups cooked couscous
½ cup finely-chopped walnuts
½ cup grated carrot
½ cup minced green onion
⅓ cup bread crumbs
4 sesame seed hamburger buns, toasted
Honey mustard
Hamburger pickles

Combine the eggs, yogurt, Worcestershire sauce, curry powder, salt and pepper in a bowl; mix well. Add the couscous, walnuts, carrot, onion and bread crumbs; mix well. Shape the mixture into 4 patties. Place the patties directly on the grill rack. Grill over a medium-high heat for 10 to 12 minutes, turning after 5 or 6 minutes. Serve on the toasted buns with the mustard and pickles.

Crab Burgers

1 cup flaked crab meat
¼ cup diced celery
2 tablespoons chopped onion
½ cup shredded Cheddar cheese
½ cup salad dressing or mayonnaise
8 hamburger buns, buttered

Combine the crab meat, celery, onion and cheese. Add the mayonnaise and mix well. Spread the mixture evenly on ½ of each hamburger bun. Top with the other ½ of the bun and broil until hot and brown.

Serves 8.

Delicious and very satisfying. Utilize the vegetable pulp leftover when juicing to create interesting combinations for patties like this.

Grilled Bison Burgers

1 pound ground bison
1-ounce envelope dry onion soup mix
1 cup chopped mushrooms
Garlic powder to taste
Salt and pepper to taste

Combine the bison and onion soup mix in a large bowl. Add the mushrooms, garlic powder, salt and pepper; mix well. Shape the mixture into 4 patties. Place the patties on a hot grill which has been sprayed with cooking spray. Remove the burgers when the juices run clear. These burgers take only minutes to cook because there is no fat.

Serves 4.

We highly recommend Kentucky bison products. This "orginal red meat" is definitely a healthy choice.

Corned Beef Burgers

12-ounce can corned beef
1 slice white bread
1 egg, slightly beaten
Dash of Worcestershire sauce
3 tablespoons butter or margarine
4 Swiss cheese slices
4 hamburger buns, toasted

Flake the corned beef with a fork. Separate the bread into soft crumbs. Combine the bread crumbs, egg, Worcestershire sauce and corned beef; mix well. Shape the mixture into 4 patties. Melt the butter in a skillet. Add the patties and brown well on both sides. Add a slice of the Swiss cheese. Serve on the buns.

Serves 4.

A nice alternative to beef.

Spicy Chicken Burgers with Creamy Horseradish

2 pounds ground chicken breast
1 cup chopped green onion
½ cup dry bread crumbs
4 teaspoons Worcestershire sauce
½ teaspoon salt
2 egg whites
8 hamburger buns, halved and lightly toasted
8 lettuce leaves

Combine the chicken, green onion, bread crumbs, Worcestershire sauce, salt and egg whites in a bowl. Form the mixture into 8 one-inch thick patties. Place the patties in a skillet. Cover and cook over a medium heat for 5 minutes or until browned. Turn the patties; cover and cook for 5 minutes or until no longer pink. Spread each bun half with 1 tablespoon of the Creamy Horseradish, 1 patty and 1 lettuce leaf. Top with the remaining half of the hamburger bun.

Serves 8.

Creamy Horseradish

2 cups sour cream
½ cup drained prepared horseradish
½ teaspoon ground black pepper
4 tablespoons white wine vinegar

Combine the sour cream, horseradish, pepper and vinegar in a small bowl and mix well. Chill, covered, for up to 3 days.

Run for the Roses Pie, Page 165
Chocolate Mint Kisses, Page 152

Fast Break Sausage and Egg Casserole, Page 54
Good Morning Grits, Page 49

deSha's Fabulous Cornbread, Page 35
Healthy and Easy White Bean Soup, Page 62

Honey Basil Chicken, Page 94
Elegant Green Beans, Page 126

Spring Asparagus Quiche, Page 51
Thunder 'n Lightning, Page 137

Decadent Chocolate Pound Cake, Page 144
Kentucky Tea Punch, Page 28

Front Porch Tea, Page 27
Grilled Bison Burgers, Page 79
Orange Almond Salad, Page 74

Hero Sandwiches

1-pound loaf French bread
Garlic butter, softened
½ pound sliced salami
¼ pound sliced Swiss cheese
2 tomatoes, sliced
Seasoned salt and pepper to taste
½ pound sliced, cooked ham
1 cucumber, thinly sliced
1 onion, thinly sliced
Lettuce
Prepared mustard

Cut the bread in half horizontally, scooping out a small portion of the center. Spread the bottom half with the garlic butter. Add one layer each of the salami , cheese and tomatoes. Season with the seasoned salt and pepper. Add one layer each of the ham, cucumber, onion and lettuce. Spread the top half of the bread with the mustard. Place the top over the meat and vegetables; secure with wooden picks. Serve heated or cold.

Turkey Brew Burgers

1½ pounds ground turkey
2 cups seasoned bread crumbs
1 cup beer
1-ounce envelope dry onion soup mix
1 cup shredded sharp Cheddar cheese
1 egg
1 tablespoon Worcestershire sauce
1 tablespoon steak sauce

Combine the turkey, bread crumbs, beer, onion soup mix, cheese, egg, Worcestershire sauce and steak sauce in a bowl; mix well. Form the mixture into 8 large patties and broil or grill.

Serves 8.

Great for the grill. A new twist.

Good idea for those watching their waistlines.

Turkey-Veggie Pita Pockets

¼ cup fat-free mayonnaise
¼ cup fat-free yogurt
1 tablespoon lemon juice
1 tablespoon Dijon mustard
1 clove garlic, minced
2 green onions, sliced
¼ teaspoon black pepper
⅛ teaspoon salt
2 pita bread rounds
8 ounces cooked turkey breast, sliced
1 medium tomato, cut into thin wedges
1 medium cucumber, scored and sliced
1 cup sprouts

Combine the mayonnaise, yogurt, lemon juice, mustard, garlic, onions, pepper and salt in a bowl; set aside. Cut the pita bread rounds in half. Divide the turkey, tomato, cucumber and sprouts evenly among the pita bread rounds. Drizzle with the mayonnaise dressing.

Serves 4.

Main Events

Pre-Derby Dinner Buffet

Honey Basil Chicken, page 94

Marinated Beef Tenderloin, page 86

Grilled Salmon with Cucumber, page 102

Elegant Green Beans, page 126

Oven-Baked Spinach, page 134

Bourbon Baked Peaches, page 140

Wild Rice

Sautéed Mushrooms, page 124

Whole Wheat Rolls, page 38

Run for the Roses Pie, page 165

Marinated Beef Tenderloin

1 cup ketchup
2 teaspoons prepared mustard
½ teaspoon Worcestershire sauce
1½ cups water
1.4-ounce envelope Italian salad dressing mix
4 to 6 pound beef tenderloin, trimmed
Watercress
Red and white grapes

Combine the ketchup, mustard, Worcestershire sauce, water and Italian salad dressing mix. Spear the meat in several places and place the meat in a resealable plastic bag. Add the marinade and seal the bag. Place the meat in a baking dish and chill for 8 hours, turning occasionally.

Drain and reserve the marinade. Place the tenderloin on a rack in a roasting pan. Bake at 425 degrees for 30 to 45 minutes, basting occasionally with the reserved marinade. Pour the marinade in a saucepan and bring to a boil. Remove the meat to a serving platter and garnish with the watercress and grapes. Serve the remaining marinade with the meat.

Serves 12 to 15.

Burrito Bake

1 pound ground beef
1.25-ounce packet taco seasoning
1 cup biscuit mix
¼ cup water
16-ounce can refried beans
1 cup thick salsa or picante sauce
1½ cups shredded mixed Cheddar and Monterey Jack cheese
Sour cream
1 sliced avocado or guacamole

Brown the ground beef in a skillet. Add the taco seasoning and cook until the meat is done; drain. Combine the biscuit mix, water and refried beans. Make a "crust" in a coated pie pan. Layer the beef, salsa and cheese. Bake at 375 degrees for 30 minutes. Serve with the sour cream and avocado or guacamole.

Serves 6 to 8.

Tasty recipe for a houseful of kids or young adults. Add a large salad for adults and you are set.

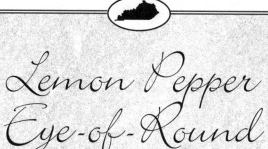

Lemon Pepper Eye-of-Round

2½ pounds eye-of-round roast
16-ounce bottle Zesty style Italian salad dressing
8-ounce bottle soy sauce
Meat tenderizer
Vegetable oil
Lemon pepper

Poke holes in the roast using a large fork. Place the roast in a heavy, resealable plastic bag. Pour in the dressing and soy sauce. Use less of these two ingredients for a smaller piece of meat, but keep the proportions the same. Chill for at least 12 hours, preferably for 24 hours. Remove the roast from the bag and discard the marinade. Sprinkle the roast with the meat tenderizer. Add enough of the vegetable oil to coat the bottom of a skillet. Heat until the oil is very hot. Add the roast, searing to a nice rich brown. Place the roast in a roasting pan. Season generously with the lemon pepper. Bake at 350 degrees, uncovered, until it reaches the desired doneness. For medium-rare, the temperature should be 145 degrees on a meat thermometer. A 2½-pound roast should take 60 to 75 minutes.

Makes 5 to 6 servings.

Company Casserole

¾ pound ground beef
¼ pound ground pork
2 medium onions, chopped
2 cups finely-chopped celery
10¾-ounce can cream of mushroom soup
10¾-ounce can tomato soup
1¼ cups water
1 teaspoon chili powder
2 cups chow mein noodles

Brown the ground beef and pork in a skillet. Add the onions and celery and cook until the vegetables are transparent. Add the mushroom soup, tomato soup, water, chili powder and 1¾ cups of the chow mein noodles. Pour the mixture into a coated baking dish. Top with the reserved chow mein noodles. Bake at 350 degrees for 45 minutes.

Savory Swiss Bliss

2 pounds eye-of-round roast
1 tablespoon butter
1-ounce envelope dry onion soup mix
½ cup chopped bell pepper
16-ounce can tomatoes, drained, reserving juice
10¾-ounce can cream of mushroom soup
¼ teaspoon salt
1 tablespoon A.1. steak sauce
1 tablespoon cornstarch

Line a 9x13-inch baking dish with aluminum foil. Place the eye-of-round roast on the foil. Add the butter, onion soup mix, pepper and tomatoes. Combine the soup, salt, tomato juice, steak sauce and cornstarch in a jar. Seal the jar and shake to mix. Pour the mixture over the steak and cover with aluminum foil. Bake at 250 degrees for 2 hours.

A dish the whole family will love!

Beans and Beef Casserole

6 slices bacon
1 pound ground beef
1 medium onion, chopped
1 cup brown sugar
½ cup ketchup
1 tablespoon mustard
15¾-ounce can pork and beans
15-ounce can lima beans
15-ounce can kidney beans

Fry the bacon in a skillet; drain. Brown the ground beef and onion in the bacon drippings; drain. Add the brown sugar, ketchup, mustard, pork and beans, lima beans and kidney beans; mix well. Pour the mixture into a large baking dish or bean pot. Crumble the bacon and stir into the mixture. Bake at 350 degrees for 30 minutes.

Christmas Party Chicken

6 cut-up chickens
3 sticks butter or margarine, melted
2 tablespoons seasoned salt
1 teaspoon pepper
2 cups orange marmalade
2 cups slivered almonds, toasted

Arrange the chicken parts, skin-side up, in a lightly-coated 9x13-inch baking dish. Combine the butter, salt and pepper in a small bowl. Brush the chicken with the melted butter. Bake at 350 degrees for 1 hour, basting once with the melted butter. Heat the marmalade in a saucepan. Remove the chicken from the oven and baste with the marmalade. Return the chicken to the oven and bake for 15 minutes. Sprinkle the top with the almonds.

Serves 24.

Oriental Chicken with Walnuts

1½ pounds chicken breasts
3 tablespoons soy sauce
2 teaspoons cornstarch
2 tablespoons dry sherry
1 teaspoon granulated sugar
1 teaspoon grated fresh ginger root
½ crushed hot red pepper
½ teaspoon salt
2 tablespoons vegetable oil
2 medium-size green peppers, cut into ¾-inch pieces
4 green onions, bias-sliced into 1-inch lengths
½ cup walnut halves

Cut the chicken into 1-inch pieces; set aside. Blend the soy sauce and cornstarch in a small bowl; stir in the sherry, sugar, ginger root, red pepper and salt. Set aside.

Pour the oil into a wok or large skillet; heat. Add the green peppers and onions and stir-fry for 2 minutes; remove. Add the walnuts and stir-fry for 1 to 2 minutes or until golden; remove. Add more oil if needed. Add ½ of the chicken and stir-fry for 2 minutes; remove. Stir-fry the remaining chicken for 2 minutes. Return the chicken to the wok. Stir the soy mixture and add to the chicken. Cook and stir until bubbly. Stir in the vegetables and walnuts; cover and cook for 1 minute.

Serves 6.

Fantastic! Serve this to guests and be prepared for compliments.

Chicken and Spinach with Pasta

9-ounce package prewashed spinach
4 skinless, boneless chicken breasts, uncooked
2 Roma tomatoes, sliced
1 cup chopped mushrooms
1.4-ounce envelope Italian salad dressing mix
Balsamic vinegar
1 cup shredded mozzarella or Parmesan cheese
1-pound package angel hair pasta or rice, cooked

Place the spinach in the bottom of a 9x13-inch baking dish. Place the chicken breasts on the top of the spinach. Place the tomatoes and mushrooms on top of the chicken. Mix the Italian salad dressing according to the package directions, substituting the balsamic vinegar for the regular vinegar. Pour the dressing over the spinach, chicken,tomatoes and mushrooms. Top with the cheese. Bake at 350 degrees for 30 minutes. Serve over the angel hair pasta or rice.

Serves 4.

Buttermilk Pecan Chicken

4 skinless, boneless chicken breasts
½ cup buttermilk
¼ cup prepared mustard
1½ cup finely-chopped pecans
Salt and pepper to taste

Cut the chicken into bite-size pieces. Combine the buttermilk and mustard in a bowl. Add the chicken pieces and coat well. Marinate for 10 minutes. Place the pecans on a plate. Remove the chicken pieces from the marinade, shaking off any excess. Dredge the chicken in the pecans. Place the chicken on a baking sheet and season with the salt and pepper. Bake at 375 degrees for 45 minutes or until the chicken is done.

Serves 6 to 8.

Savory Chicken Scallop

4 cups cooked, diced chicken
4 cups dry bread crumbs
2 cups cooked rice
¾ cup chopped celery
¾ cup chopped onion
⅓ cup chopped pimento
½ teaspoon salt
Pepper to taste
1½ teaspoons poultry seasoning
1½ cups milk
4 eggs, slightly beaten
1½ cups chicken broth
Two 10¾-ounce cans cream of mushroom soup
½ cup milk
1 cup sour cream

Nice dish to make ahead and refrigerate.

Combine the chicken, bread crumbs, rice, celery, onion, pimento, salt, pepper, poultry seasoning, 1½ cups of milk, eggs and chicken broth in a large bowl; mix well. Spoon the mixture into a coated 9x13-inch baking dish. Bake at 350 degrees for 55 minutes or until a knife inserted comes out clean. Cut into squares and set aside. Combine the soup, ½ cup of milk and sour cream. Heat in a saucepan and serve over the chicken squares.

Honey Basil Chicken

1 cup raspberry vinegar
3 tablespoons Dijon mustard
2 tablespoons soy sauce
2 tablespoons honey
2 tablespoons minced basil
½ teaspoon dried thyme
Pinch of ground pepper
4 boneless, skinless chicken breasts, chopped

Combine the vinegar, mustard, soy sauce, honey, basil, thyme and pepper in a shallow baking dish. Add the chicken and marinate for 15 minutes. Transfer the chicken into a skillet and brown. Add the marinade and simmer. Serve over cooked rice.

Serves 4.

Chicken and Dumplings

4 to 5 chicken breasts
1 teaspoon salt
¼ teaspoon pepper
⅛ teaspoon poultry seasoning
1 tablespoon butter
1 carrot, chopped
1 celery stalk, chopped
14-ounce can chicken broth
10¾-ounce cream of chicken soup
1½ soup cans water
Three to four 12-ounce cans refrigerated biscuits, torn

Combine the chicken, salt, pepper, poultry seasoning, butter, carrot and celery in a large stockpot. Cover with water and simmer for 30 minutes or until the chicken is tender. Remove the chicken and strain. Add the chicken broth, soup and water to the stock. Season to taste. Bring the mixture to a boil and drop the biscuits into the broth. Gently press the biscuits in the broth to cover. Cover and simmer for 8 to 10 minutes. Serve with the chicken breasts or tear the meat and add to the dumplings.

Delicious Chicken

½ cup flour
Salt and pepper to taste
8 chicken breasts, flattened
2 tablespoons olive oil
3 tablespoons butter
½ green pepper, thinly sliced
½ red pepper, thinly sliced
2 cloves garlic
8 large mushrooms, sliced
2 tomatoes, peeled and chopped
4 ounces white wine
2 tablespoons chopped parsley
½ cup chopped olives

Combine the flour, salt and pepper. Dredge the chicken in the flour mixture. Heat the olive oil and butter in a large skillet and sauté the chicken until brown. Place the chicken in a 10x15-inch baking dish. Add the peppers, garlic and mushrooms and sauté for 4 minutes. Add the tomatoes and wine and simmer for 10 minutes. Pour the mixture over the chicken. Bake at 325 degrees for 1 to 1½ hours. Garnish with the parsley and olives.

Spicy Chicken

23 ounces vermicelli spaghetti
3 cups cooked chicken, reserving broth
8-ounce can mushrooms
2 large bell peppers, chopped
2 large onions, chopped
1 stick margarine
10-ounce can tomatoes with green chiles
1 pound Velveeta cheese, cut into 1-inch chunks

Cook the spaghetti in the reserved chicken broth; drain. Sauté the mushrooms, peppers and onions in the margarine in a skillet. Combine the chicken, spaghetti, tomatoes, Velveeta cheese and vegetables in a 9x13-inch baking dish. Bake at 350 degrees until hot.

Serves 6 to 8.

Pork Tenderloin with Cranberries

1-pound pork tenderloin, cut into ½-inch slices
3 tablespoons olive or vegetable oil
1 onion, chopped
1 clove garlic, minced
4 tablespoons sugar
¾ cup apple juice
½ cup cranberry juice
½ cup fresh or frozen cranberries
2 teaspoons Dijon mustard
½ teaspoon rosemary

Cook the tenderloin in the oil in a skillet for 3 to 4 minutes until the meat is browned. Remove the pork from the skillet. Add the onion, garlic and sugar.

Sauté until the onion is caramelized. Stir in the apple juice, cranberry juice, cranberries, mustard and rosemary. Bring the mixture to a boil. Add the pork; reduce the heat and simmer, covered, for 30 minutes.

Corn Sausage Loaf

2 eggs, well beaten
14¾-ounce can cream-style corn
15¼-ounce can whole kernel corn, drained
1½ pounds lean sausage, uncooked
1 cup bread crumbs
⅛ teaspoon pepper
1 teaspoon salt
6 tablespoons ketchup

Combine the eggs, corn, sausage, bread crumbs, pepper and salt; mix well. Place the mixture into a coated baking dish. Cover the top with the ketchup. Bake at 350 degrees for 1 hour.

Marinated Grilled Pork

½ large onion
2 cloves garlic
1 teaspoon pepper
6 tablespoons lime juice
½ cup soy sauce
¼ cup dark molasses
½ cup salad oil
2½ pounds boneless pork

Place the onion, garlic, pepper, lime juice, soy sauce, molasses and oil in a blender container. Process until the onion is finely chopped. Pour the mixture over the pork and marinate, chilled, for 3 to 4 hours or overnight. Remove the pork from the marinade and grill.

This recipe was handed down from "Mom" and enjoyed throughout the years.

Honey Herb Grilled Pork Roast

1 cup beer
½ cup honey
½ cup Dijon mustard
¼ cup olive oil
½ small onion, finely chopped
1 clove garlic, minced
2 teaspoons dried rosemary
½ teaspoon salt
¼ teaspoon ground black pepper
3 pounds pork loin roast
1 large yellow onion, thinly sliced

Combine the beer, honey, mustard, oil, chopped onion, garlic, rosemary, salt and pepper in a bowl; blend to make a marinade. Place the pork in a resealable plastic bag. Add the marinade and seal. Marinate, chilled, for 4 hours. Remove the pork from the marinade. Wrap the pork in aluminum foil and grill over a medium heat for 1½ hours. use the marinade for frequent basting. Add the sliced onion to the pork packet during the last 15 minutes of grilling.

Easy Baked Country Ham

Country ham slices, sliced ¼-inch thick

Wrap the country ham slices in aluminum foil and place the foil packet on a baking sheet. Bake at 350 degrees for about 1 hour.

The country ham is tender this way and you avoid the mess of frying.

Sweet and Sour Pork Chops

6 pork chops, ¾ to 1-inch thick
2 tablespoons shortening
1 teaspoon salt
¼ teaspoon pepper
1 cup thinly-sliced carrots
½ cup lemon juice
¼ cup honey
½ cup chopped onion
1 tablespoon soy sauce
1 teaspoon instant beef bouillon
20 ounces pineapple chunks, drained, reserving juice
3 teaspoons cornstarch
6 green pepper rings

Brown the chops in the shortening in a skillet. Place the chops in a coated 3-quart baking dish. Season with the salt and pepper. Add the carrots. Combine the lemon juice, honey, onion, soy sauce, bouillon and ½ of the reserved pineapple juice in a saucepan. Combine the cornstarch and the remaining pineapple juice in a cup and add to the lemon mixture. Cook, stirring constantly, until thickened. Pour the lemon mixture over the chops. Bake, covered, at 350 degrees for 50 to 60 minutes or until the chops are tender. Add the pineapple chunks and pepper rings. Cover and bake for 10 minutes.

A nice blend of crab meat and shrimp.

Seafood Wild Rice Casserole

6-ounce package wild rice
⅓ cup minced onion
1 cup chopped green pepper
1 cup chopped celery
2 cups sliced fresh mushrooms
1 pound fresh or frozen crab meat
1 pound shrimp, cooked and peeled
Three 10¾-ounce cans cream of mushroom soup

Cook the rice according to the package directions. Add the onion, pepper, celery and mushrooms to the cooked rice and mix well. Add the crab meat, shrimp and soup; mix well. Pour the mixture into a lightly coated 4-quart baking dish. Bake, uncovered, at 325 degrees for 1 hour.

Serves 6.

Shrimp and Artichoke Casserole

For the sauce:

3½ tablespoons butter
4½ tablespoons flour
¾ cup milk
¾ cup heavy whipping cream
Salt and white pepper to taste
¼ cup dry sherry
1 tablespoon Worcestershire sauce

For the casserole:

3 tablespoons butter
8-ounce package cremini or white button mushrooms, sliced
14-ounce can artichoke hearts, cut into quarters
1 pound raw shrimp, peeled and deveined
½ cup freshly-grated Parmesan cheese

Artichokes and Parmesan cheese are terrific complements to the subtle sweetness of shrimp.

Melt the 3½ tablespoons butter in a saucepan or in the top of a double boiler over a low heat. Add the flour, stirring constantly, until it forms a smooth paste. Add the milk and cream, gradually, when the paste barely begins to bubble. Cook over a medium-low heat until the sauce thickens. Season with the salt and white pepper. Remove the pan from the heat and stir in the sherry and Worcestershire sauce; set aside.

Melt the 3 tablespoons butter in a skillet over a medium heat. Add the mushrooms and cook for 4 to 5 minutes or until the mushrooms are soft and release some of their liquid. Place the artichoke hearts and the shrimp in a lightly coated 9x13-inch baking dish. Add the mushrooms. Pour the sauce over the top and sprinkle with the Parmesan cheese. Bake at 375 degrees for 20 to 30 minutes or until bubbly and golden on top. Serve at once over cooked rice or pasta.

Serves 4.

Shrimp with Smoked Salmon and Dill

6 large shrimp, peeled and deveined
Salt and white pepper to taste
½ ounce olive oil
½ ounce dry white wine
2 lemon wedges
½ teaspoon finely-chopped fresh dill
2 ounces whipping cream
½ ounce smoked salmon, coarsely chopped
Rice pilaf or pasta, cooked

Season the shrimp with the salt and white pepper. Sauté the shrimp in the olive oil in a skillet over a medium heat. Remove the shrimp from the skillet and keep warm. Add the white wine, juice from 1 lemon wedge and dill to the skillet; bring to a simmer. Add the cream and salmon. Simmer until the liquid thickens slightly. Return the shrimp to the pan and coat with the sauce. Serve the shrimp with the remaining lemon wedge and the rice pilaf or pasta.

Makes 1 serving.

Grilled Salmon with Cucumber Sauce

1 tablespoon butter
3 tablespoons olive oil
2 tablespoons dill pickle juice
½ lime or lemon
1 tablespoon garlic powder
Black pepper to taste
6 salmon fillets

Combine the butter, oil and pickle juice in an ovenproof bowl. Squeeze the lime or lemon juice into the mixture. Microwave the mixture until the butter melts. Add the garlic powder and pepper; stir. Brush the fillets with the mixture. Place the fillets in a grilling basket or on an aluminum foil-covered grill rack. Grill over a medium-low heat until the fillets flake easily. Do not overcook as salmon dries out quickly. Serve with Cucumber Sauce.

Serves 6.

Cucumber Sauce

1 medium cucumber
½ cup sour cream
¼ cup mayonnaise
1 tablespoon snipped parsley
2 teaspoons grated onion
2 teaspoons vinegar
⅓ teaspoon salt
Dash of pepper

Halve the cucumber lengthwise and seed. Process the cucumber in a food processor to make 1 cup; do not drain. Combine the cucumber, sour cream, mayonnaise, parsley, onion, vinegar, salt and pepper. Cover and chill until ready to serve.

Makes 1½ cups.

Easy sauce to make and serve with any seafood.

Everybody has leftover turkey after Thanksgiving dinner—often more than can be used in a safe amount of time. Refrigerated sliced turkey from the big dinner should be used within three to four days, according to current safe-food-handling guidelines. After the obligatory turkey sandwiches on the Friday after Thanksgiving, we turn to this recipe to take care of the leftovers in a delicious way.

Twisted Turkey

3 ounces cream cheese, at room temperature
3 tablespoons melted butter, divided
2 cups cooked, cubed turkey
¼ teaspoon salt
¼ teaspoon freshly-ground black pepper
2 tablespoons milk
1 tablespoon chopped fresh chives
1 tablespoon chopped pimento
8-ounce can refrigerated crescent rolls
¼ cup dry bread crumbs

Blend the cream cheese and 2 tablespoons of the butter with a spoon, mixing well. Add the turkey, salt, pepper, milk, chives and pimento; mix well. Separate the crescent rolls into four rectangular sections, pressing the perforations to seal. Spoon about ½ cup of the turkey mixture onto the center of each rectangle. Pull up the sides of the rolls, twisting the tops and pinching the side seams together to seal the turkey mixture inside. Place the bundles on a foil-lined baking sheet. Brush the top of each with the remaining butter. Sprinkle the bread crumbs on top. Bake at 350 degrees for 20 to 25 minutes or until golden.

Makes 3 to 4 light lunch servings or 2 to 3 dinner servings.

Quail in White Wine Sauce

4 tablespoons butter
1 medium onion, chopped
10 to 12 dressed quail
Salt and freshly-ground black pepper to taste
2 teaspoons dried parsley flakes
2 teaspoons light-colored Worcestershire sauce

¼ **teaspoon dried thyme leaves**
½ **cup white wine**
1 cup chicken broth
Shake and Blend flour

Melt the butter in a skillet over a medium heat. Add the onion and sauté the onion until transparent. Season the quail with the salt and pepper. Add the quail to the pan, browning on both sides. Add the parsley flakes, Worcestershire sauce and thyme. Reduce the heat to a simmer. Arrange the quail breast sides up. Add the wine and chicken broth. Reduce the heat and cover. Cook for 1 to 1½ hours or until the quail are tender and cooked through. Push the quail to the edges of the pan and sprinkle a small amount of the flour into the sauce, stirring to thicken. Remove the quail from the pan when the gravy is the consistency you prefer. Arrange the quail on serving plates, spooning the gravy over them.

Serves 4 to 6.

Good and Easy Venison

6-pound venison hindquarter or loin roast
6 to 8 slices bacon
Two 1-ounce envelopes dry onion soup mix
2 to 3 bay leaves

Place the venison in a roasting pan. Place the bacon slices on top of the venison. Sprinkle the dry soup mix over the top. Pour 1 to 2 cups of water in the bottom of the roasting pan and add the bay leaves. Cover and bake at 350 degrees for 3 to 4 hours, basting occasionally. Use a carving fork inserted into the thickest part to test the tenderness of the meat. Use the pan drippings to make a gravy.

Serves 6 to 8.

You can use venison straight from the freezer for this recipe – no thawing needed.

Venison is notoriously dry, but this recipe avoids that problem. We like this roast on the Thanksgiving dinner table, right next to the turkey.

Bison Meat Loaf

1 pound ground bison
1 egg, beaten
1-ounce envelope dry onion soup mix
2 cups bread crumbs or oats
½ cup ketchup
¼ cup chopped green pepper
Salt and pepper to taste
⅛ cup red wine vinegar
⅓ cup brown sugar
¼ cup ketchup

Combine the bison, egg and soup mix in a large bowl. Add the crumbs, ½ cup ketchup and green pepper. Season with the salt and pepper; mix well. Shape the mixture into a loaf. Place the loaf in an ovenproof dish. Bake, uncovered, at 325 degrees for 25 minutes. Combine the vinegar, brown sugar and ketchup; mix well. Spoon the sauce over the meat loaf and bake for 15 minutes.

Serves 4.

Wonderful alternative to beef. Meat loaf may be considered "old fashioned" but everyone loves this. Leftovers are yummy for sandwiches.

One
Dishing

After the Game Buffet

Kentucky Burgoo

1 chicken
2-pound beef chuck roast
1½-pound lamb shoulder
½ veal shoulder
1 ham bone
Salt and pepper to taste
½ bunch celery, chopped
½ pound carrots, chopped
1½ pounds green beans, chopped
3 green peppers, chopped
3 medium onions, chopped
4 potatoes, chopped
½ head cabbage, shredded
16-ounce bag frozen peas, thawed
16-ounce bag frozen sliced okra, thawed
16-ounce bag frozen corn, thawed
Three 15-ounce cans tomatoes
5 ounces Worcestershire sauce
10 ounces ketchup
¼ cup vinegar

Place the chicken, beef, lamb, veal and ham bone in a large stockpot, cover the meats with water and season with the salt and pepper. Cook until the meats are tender and stringy. Remove the meat. Pull the meat from the bones. Return the meat to the broth. Add the celery, carrots, green beans, peppers, onions, potatoes and cabbage. Add the peas, okra, corn, tomatoes, Worcestershire sauce, ketchup and vinegar. Cook until the vegetables are tender. Serve the burgoo in mugs along with fresh bread.

An old Kentucky tradition. Served at many celebrations and functions. Great for a large crowd.

Baked Beef Stew

14½-ounce can diced tomatoes, undrained
1 cup water
3 tablespoons quick-cooking tapioca
2 teaspoons sugar
1½ teaspoons salt
½ teaspoon pepper
2 pounds lean beef, cut into 1-inch cubes
4 carrots, cut into chunks
3 potatoes, peeled and quartered
2 celery ribs, cut into ¾-inch chunks
1 onion, cut into chunks
1 slice bread, cubed

Combine the tomatoes, water, tapioca, sugar, salt and pepper in a large bowl. Add the beef, carrots, potatoes, celery, onion and bread; mix well. Pour the mixture into a coated 9x13-inch or 3-quart baking dish. Cover and bake at 375 degrees for 1¾ to 2 hours or until the meat and vegetables are tender. Serve in bowls.

Serves 6 to 8.

The Southerner's twist on a rueben sandwich.

Rueben Casserole

27-ounce can sauerkraut
½ cup Thousand Island salad dressing
½ cup mayonnaise
12-ounce can corned beef, cut in slices
1 cup shredded Swiss cheese
2 slices buttered pumpernickel bread, cubed

Combine the sauerkraut, dressing and mayonnaise. Pour the mixture into a 2-quart baking dish. Add one layer of the corned beef and one layer of the Swiss cheese. Top with the pumpernickel cubes. Bake at 300 degrees for 30 minutes.

Beef-Cabbage Casserole

3-pound head cabbage
1 cup uncooked rice
1 pound ground beef, browned
1 teaspoon salt
½ teaspoon pepper
1 small onion, grated
Two 8-ounce cans tomato sauce

Cut the cabbage into eighths, removing the core. Cook the cabbage in boiling water for 5 to 6 minutes; drain. Cook the rice according to the package directions. Combine the rice, beef, salt, pepper and onion in a large bowl. Place a layer of the cabbage in the bottom of a 3-quart baking dish. Place a layer of the meat mixture on top. Add another layer of the cabbage and another layer of the meat mixture. Spread the tomato sauce on top. Bake at 350 degrees for 1 hour. Add water, if needed, as it cooks to keep the casserole from sticking.

Serves 8.

Stuffed Cabbage

1 large head cabbage, core removed
1½ pounds ground chuck
2 onions, chopped
2 to 3 cloves garlic, chopped
1 tablespoon vegetable oil
1 cup rice
2 cups water
½ teaspoon salt
½ teaspoon pepper
2 eggs, beaten
3 tablespoons tomato sauce
14½-ounce can sauerkraut
3 to 4 strips bacon, uncooked
16-ounce can tomato sauce

Steam the cabbage leaves in boiling water. Brown the ground chuck in a skillet; drain. Sauté the onions and garlic in the vegetable oil in a skillet. Add the ground chuck. Cook the rice in the water until partially done. Drain the rice and add to the ground chuck mixture. Add the salt, pepper, eggs and the 3 tablespoons of tomato sauce; mix well. Place the mixture, by tablespoonfuls, into the cabbage leaves. Roll the leaves and fold the ends.

Place ½ of the can of sauerkraut on the bottom of a Dutch oven or stockpot. Place the cabbage rolls on top. Top with the remaining sauerkraut. Chop any remaining cabbage and place on top of the sauerkraut. Place the bacon on top. Cover with the 16 ounces tomato sauce and add enough water to completely cover. Cover and simmer over a low heat for 2 hours.

Chicken Tetrazzini

¾ cup butter
¾ cup flour
4 cups chicken broth
3 cups half-and-half
½ cup dry sherry
¼ teaspoon nutmeg
2 teaspoons salt
¾ teaspoon pepper
½ teaspoon garlic salt
1 pound spaghetti, cooked al dente and drained
6 cups diced, cooked chicken
4-ounce can sliced mushrooms, drained
1½ cups grated Parmesan cheese
Paprika

Melt the butter in a saucepan over a medium heat. Add the flour and cook for 1 minute, stirring constantly. Add the chicken broth, half-and-half, sherry, nutmeg, salt, pepper and garlic salt; cook until thick, smooth and bubbly. Layer ¼ of the spaghetti, ¼ of the chicken, ½ of the mushrooms, ¼ of the sauce, ¼ of the spaghetti, ¼ of the chicken, ¼ of the sauce and ½ of the Parmesan cheese in two coated 9x13-inch baking dishes. Sprinkle the tops lightly with the paprika. Bake at 350 degrees for 30 to 40 minutes.

Serves 12.

A wonderful make-ahead recipe that's sure to be a family favorite.

Family Chicken and Noodle Casserole

4 to 5 green onions, chopped
2 tablespoons butter
5 to 6 chicken breasts, cooked and chopped, reserving broth
23 ounces fettuccini
2 tablespoons butter
1 cup mayonnaise
1 cup sour cream
10¾-ounce can cream of mushroom soup
1½ teaspoons Dijon mustard
3 tablespoons dry sherry
6 ounces grated Cheddar cheese
Freshly-grated Parmesan cheese

Sauté the green onions in the 2 tablespoons of butter. Combine the onions and chicken. Cook the fettuccini according to the package directions, using the reserved chicken broth instead of water. Drain the fettuccini and toss with the 2 tablespoons of butter.

Combine the mayonnaise, sour cream, soup, mustard, sherry and Cheddar cheese; mix well. Place the fettuccini in a 9x13-inch baking dish. Cover with the chicken mixture. Top with the sauce. Sprinkle generously with the Parmesan cheese. Bake at 350 degrees for 35 minutes.

Serves 6.

Shrimp Milano

1 pound peeled shrimp, cooked and drained
2 cups sliced mushrooms
1 cup green pepper strips
1 garlic clove, minced
¼ cup margarine
¾ pound Velveeta cheese, cubed
¾ cup whipping cream
½ teaspoon dill weed
⅓ cup grated Parmesan cheese
8 ounces fettuccini, cooked and drained

Sauté the shrimp, mushrooms, pepper and garlic in the margarine in a large skillet. Reduce the heat. Add the Velveeta cheese, cream and dill. Stir until the cheese is melted. Stir in the Parmesan cheese. Add the fettuccini. Toss lightly.

Serves 6.

Catfish Dinner

Fishermen and non-fishermen will love this recipe. A favorite of the lakes area.

1 red bell pepper, cut into strips
1 carrot, cut into strips
1 zucchini, cut into strips
3 tablespoons butter, melted
8 ounces catfish fillets, cut into 2-inch strips
14-ounce can artichoke hearts, drained and quartered
⅔ cup whipping cream
8 ounces angel hair pasta, cooked and drained
½ cup grated Parmesan cheese

Sauté the pepper, carrot and zucchini in the butter in a skillet until tender. Remove the vegetables and add the catfish fillets. Sauté until tender. Return the vegetables to the skillet. Add the artichokes and whipping cream. Cook over a low heat until heated through. Add the pasta and Parmesan cheese; toss gently.

Serves 4.

Baked Fish Casserole

3 medium potatoes, diced
2 large carrots, sliced
1½ to 2 pounds orange roughy fillets
Butter to taste
Lemon juice to taste
Garlic powder to taste
Seasoned salt and pepper to taste
8-ounce can green peas, drained
8-ounce can whole kernel corn, drained
14½-ounce can whole tomatoes, drained and chopped
2 to 3 medium onions, sliced
1 teaspoon sugar

Boil the potatoes and carrots in a saucepan for 5 minutes; drain. Place the fish on 2 layers of heavy duty aluminum foil. Season with the butter, lemon juice, garlic powder, seasoned salt and pepper. Add the peas, corn, tomatoes and onions. Sprinkle with the sugar. Top with aluminum foil and wrap tightly. Place the packet on a baking sheet. Bake at 375 degrees for 1 hour and 20 minutes.

Serves 4.

The South's version of the North's fish boil.

A

wonderful

alternative to

the traditional

lasagna and

a crowd

pleaser too.

White Lasagna for a Christmas Buffet

1 onion, chopped
2 tablespoons butter
2 tablespoons flour
2 cups chicken broth
10-ounce jar Alfredo sauce
10-ounce box frozen, chopped spinach, thawed and well drained
12 lasagna noodles, cooked
8-ounce package sliced mozzarella cheese
8-ounce container ricotta or cottage cheese
3 cups chopped, cooked chicken breast
Parmesan cheese

Sauté the onion in the butter in a skillet. Add the flour, stirring until blended. Slowly add the chicken broth; mixing well. Cook until slightly thickened. Add the Alfredo sauce and spinach. Spoon enough of the sauce to cover the bottom of a lightly-coated 9x13-inch baking dish. Layer the noodles, mozzarella cheese, ricotta cheese, chicken and sauce, finishing with the sauce on top. Sprinkle with the Parmesan cheese. Bake at 350 degrees for 30 to 45 minutes.

Serves 8 to 10.

Besides

Harvest Time Family Dinner

Pork Tenderloin with Cranberries, page 96

Hot Cabbage Creole, page 135

Oven-Baked Potatoes, page 128

Roasted Vegetables, page 126

Shoe Peg Corn Casserole, page 133

Praline Cheesecake, page 149

Butter Rum Apple Cake, page 145

Mushrooms Florentine

1 pound fresh mushrooms
1 tablespoon vegetable oil
1 teaspoon salt
¼ cup chopped onion
¼ cup melted butter or margarine
Two 10-ounce packages frozen, chopped spinach,
lightly cooked and drained
1 cup grated Cheddar cheese
Garlic salt to taste

Sauté the mushrooms in the oil in a skillet until brown. Combine the salt, onion, butter and spinach. Spread the spinach mixture in a 10-inch baking dish. Sprinkle the spinach with ½ cup of the grated cheese. Place the mushrooms on top of the spinach; season with the garlic salt. Cover with the remaining cheese. Chill until baking time. Bake at 350 degrees for 20 minutes, if just prepared, or 35 minutes if chilled.

Serves 6 to 8.

Sautéed Mushrooms

1 tablespoon olive oil
3 tablespoons butter
16 to 18 ounces mushrooms, sliced
3 tablespoons Worcestershire sauce
1½ tablespoons soy sauce
Seasoned salt to taste
Garlic powder to taste
Black pepper to taste
4 to 5 drops Tabasco sauce

Heat the olive oil and butter in a skillet. Add the mushrooms, Worcestershire sauce, soy sauce, seasoned salt, garlic powder, pepper and Tabasco sauce; stir. Sauté over a low heat for 15 to 20 minutes.

Potluck Baked Beans

1 pound bacon
Two 1-pound cans pork and beans, undrained
1-pound can kidney beans, undrained
1-pound can butter beans, undrained
1-pound can barbecue beans, undrained
1-pound can great northern beans, undrained
¼ cup minced onion
¾ cup brown sugar
½ cup white vinegar
1 teaspoon dry mustard
1 teaspoon garlic salt

Cut the bacon into inch-size pieces; cook the bacon until almost done, but not crisp. Pour off all but ¼ cup of the bacon grease. Place the pork and beans, kidney beans, butter beans, barbecue beans, northern beans, bacon and the reserved bacon grease in a 9x13-inch baking dish. Add the onion, brown sugar, vinegar, mustard and garlic salt. Mix well, being careful not to mash the beans. Bake, uncovered, at 350 degrees for 2½ hours.

Serves 12.

"Old timey" recipe with a flavorful taste. Perfect dish for a picnic or reunion.

Elegant Green Beans

Two 14½-ounce cans whole green beans
2 slices bacon
½ cup brown sugar
Garlic salt to taste
2 tablespoons butter, sliced

Rinse the beans in cold water; drain. Place the beans in a coated baking dish. Cut the bacon into small pieces and place on top of the beans. Spread the brown sugar on top. Season with the garlic salt and dot with the butter. Bake, uncovered, at 350 degrees for 30 minutes, stirring often.

Serves 6.

Roasted Vegetables

½ head broccoli, separated into florets
½ head cauliflower, separated into florets
2 large onions, cut into wedges
3 carrots, peeled and sliced
4 potatoes, skin on, cut into wedges
½ cup olive oil
Tangy honey Shake 'n Bake

Combine the broccoli, cauliflower, onions, carrots and potatoes in a bowl. Add the oil and mix until the vegetables are coated. Place the vegetables in a single layer on a large coated baking sheet. Sprinkle the vegetables lightly with the Shake 'n Bake. Bake at 400 degrees for 40 minutes or until the vegetables are done.

Tomato Pie

12-ounce can refrigerated biscuits
6 to 8 tomatoes, peeled and sliced
¼ to ½ cup chopped green pepper
¼ to ½ cup chopped onion
⅔ cup mayonnaise
1 cup shredded mozzarella or Swiss cheese

Press the biscuits into a pie plate to form a crust. Cover the crust with the sliced tomatoes. Sauté the pepper and onion in a skillet until the vegetables are soft. Place the vegetables over the tomatoes. Combine the mayonnaise and cheese. Spread the mixture over the top of the tomatoes. Bake at 350 degrees for 40 to 50 minutes. Cool for 30 minutes before serving.

Serves 8.

Easy, easy and so delicious.

Oven Fried Sweet Potatoes

2 large sweet potatoes, peeled and cut into ¾-inch thick slices
3 tablespoons oil
¾ teaspoon cinnamon
¾ teaspoon ginger
½ teaspoon salt
¼ teaspoon pepper

Combine the sweet potatoes, oil, cinnamon, ginger, salt and pepper in a bowl. Toss the mixture to coat. Arrange the potatoes in a single layer on a heated baking sheet. Bake at 450 degrees for 30 to 35 minutes or until the potatoes are crisp on the outside and tender inside.

Potato Casserole

6 to 8 medium potatoes, cooked and diced
1 small onion, chopped
2 slices white bread, cubed
½ green pepper, chopped
2-ounce jar pimento, drained
½ pound Velveeta cheese, cubed
1 tablespoon dried parsley flakes
½ cup butter
½ cup milk
½ cup crushed cornflakes

Combine the potatoes, onion, bread, pepper, pimento, cheese and parsley. Place the mixture in a coated 9x13-inch baking dish. Melt the butter in a saucepan. Add the milk and mix well. Pour the mixture over the potato mixture. Top with the cornflakes. Bake at 375 degrees for 30 minutes.

Oven Baked Potatoes

8 large unpeeled potatoes
½ cup oil
2 tablespoons grated Parmesan cheese
1 teaspoon salt
½ teaspoon garlic powder
½ teaspoon paprika
¼ teaspoon black pepper

Cut each potato into eight wedges. Arrange the potatoes on a baking sheet. Combine the oil, cheese, salt, garlic powder, paprika and pepper; mix well. Brush the mixture over the potatoes. Bake at 375 degrees for 45 minutes or until the potatoes are golden brown and tender, basting occasionally.

Serves 8.

Pickled Beets

4 quarts whole beets
3 cups vinegar
2 cups water
2½ cups sugar
2 teaspoons allspice
3-inch cinnamon stick
½ teaspoon whole cloves
1 teaspoon salt

Cook the beets until tender. Peel off the skins. Combine the vinegar, water, sugar, allspice, cinnamon stick, cloves and salt in a saucepan. Bring to a boil, reduce the heat and simmer for 15 minutes. Add the beets and simmer for 5 minutes. Remove the beets and pack into hot sterilized jars. Bring the syrup to a boil and pour over the beets. Add hot vinegar if the beets are not completely covered. Seal immediately.

Makes 4 quarts.

Eggplant Parmigiana

1 egg
1½ tablespoons milk
Dash of salt and pepper
1½ cups flour
1 large eggplant, peeled and sliced
Vegetable oil
26-ounce jar spaghetti sauce
Salt and pepper to taste
½ teaspoon garlic powder
¼ cup grated Romano cheese
¼ cup grated mozzarella cheese

Combine the egg, milk, salt and pepperin a bowl; whip until foamy. Pour the flour into a separate bowl. Dip the eggplant slices into the flour, then the milk mixture and again into the flour. Pour enough of the vegetable oil into a large skillet to slightly cover the bottom; heat. Brown the eggplant slices on each side. Remove the slices and place them on a paper towel. Place the slices in a large baking dish in a single layer. Cover with the spaghetti sauce. Season with the salt and pepper and garlic powder. Spread the grated cheeses over the top. Bake at 375 degrees for 25 to 30 minutes.

Garden Stuffed Yellow Squash

4 to 5 medium yellow squash
½ cup chopped green pepper
1 medium tomato, chopped
1 medium onion, chopped
2 slices bacon, fried crisp and crumbled
½ cup shredded Cheddar cheese
½ teaspoon salt
½ teaspoon pepper
½ teaspoon butter

Simmer the whole squash in a saucepan in enough water to cover for 8 minutes or until tender. Drain and slightly cool. Slice each squash in half and remove the seeds. Combine the green pepper, tomato, onion, bacon, cheese, salt and pepper; mix well. Spoon the mixture into the squash shells. Dot each shell with a pat of the butter. Bake at 400 degrees for 20 minutes.

Serves 8 .

In the summertime when the garden is running over with squash— freeze it! Rinse, drain and slice the squash and drop it in a resealable plastic bag and freeze. In the winter, when it's time to make soups and stews, pull out those bags and add the fresh vegetable.

Sunny Summer Squash Casserole

2 tablespoons butter
¼ cup crumbled butter crackers
¼ cup chopped pecans
¼ cup water
½ teaspoon salt
1 pound yellow squash, sliced
¼ cup mayonnaise
1 egg, beaten
½ cup shredded Cheddar cheese
2 tablespoons melted butter
1½ teaspoons sugar
¼ to ½ teaspoon minced onion

Melt the the 2 tablespoons of butter in a 1-quart baking dish in the microwave. Add the cracker crumbs and pecans and microwave for 1 minute. Stir the mixture and microwave again for 1 minute. Pour the crumb mixture onto waxed paper; set aside. Combine the water, salt and squash in the baking dish. Cover and microwave for 4 minutes. Stir the squash and microwave for 4 to 6 minutes or until the squash is tender. Drain the juice. Combine the mayonnaise, egg, cheese, the 2 tablespoons of melted butter, sugar and minced onion in a bowl. Pour the mayonnaise mixture over the squash and gently mix. Top with the crumb mixture. Microwave for 2 to 4 minutes or until the center is set. Allow the casserole to stand for 5 minutes before serving.

Spanish Corn

2 tablespoons chopped green pepper
2 tablespoons chopped onion
¼ cup butter
2 cups fresh or canned corn
2 cups fresh or canned tomatoes
1 teaspoon salt
Dash of sugar
¼ teaspoon pepper
¼ teaspoon celery salt
1 cup buttered bread crumbs

Sauté the pepper and onion in the butter in a skillet. Add the corn, tomatoes, salt, sugar, pepper and celery salt. Pour the mixture into a coated 1½-quart baking dish. Top with the bread crumbs. Bake at 350 degrees for 45 minutes.

Serves 6.

Shoe Peg Corn Casserole

½ cup milk
2 to 3 tablespoons margarine
6 ounces cream cheese
24 ounces Shoe Peg corn, well drained
2 ounces chopped green chiles
Dash of black pepper
½ cup grated cheddar cheese

Combine the milk, margarine and cream cheese in a 2-quart baking dish. Microwave until smooth. Add the corn, chiles and pepper; mix well. Top with the grated cheese. Bake 350 degrees for 15 minutes.

Oven-Baked Spinach

4 tablespoons margarine
3 tablespoons cornstarch
1 teaspoon salt
¼ teaspoon pepper
2 cups milk
Two 10-ounce packages frozen spinach or 2 cups canned spinach, drained
2 hard-boiled eggs, chopped
4 strips crisp bacon, crumbled
½ to 1 cup bread crumbs

Melt the margarine in a saucepan. Add the cornstarch, salt and pepper; blend well. Remove the saucepan from the heat and slowly stir in the milk. Return the saucepan to the heat and cook until the mixture thickens, stirring constantly. Remove the saucepan from the heat and set aside. Alternate layers of the spinach, bacon and eggs in a coated baking dish. Cover each layer with a small amount of the sauce, ending with the sauce on the top. Sprinkle the mixture with the bread crumbs. Bake at 375 degrees for 15 minutes or until the mixture bubbles.

A different and delicious way to serve this vegetable!

Baked Asparagus

Two 10½-ounce cans asparagus, drained
8 hard-boiled eggs, diced
Two 10¾-ounce cans cream of mushroom soup
½ to 1 cup milk
1 stick butter
2 cups cracker crumbs

Place the asparagus and eggs in a 2-quart baking dish. Combine the soup and milk in a bowl. Pour the soup mixture over the asparagus and eggs. Melt the butter and top with the cracker crumbs. Bake at 350 degrees for 30 minutes or until the casserole bubbles.

Hot Cabbage Creole

1½ heads cabbage, chopped
3 large tomatoes, quartered
2 green peppers, sliced
1 large red onion, quartered
½ pound uncooked bacon, chopped
1½ tablespoons salt
½ teaspoon black pepper
¼ teaspoon cayenne pepper
¾ cup brown sugar
2 quarts tomato sauce
½ cup vinegar

Place the cabbage, tomatoes, peppers, onion and bacon in a large stockpot. Add the salt, black pepper, cayenne pepper, brown sugar, tomato sauce and vinegar. Cook over a medium heat, stirring occasionally, until the cabbage is tender.

A new idea for an old favorite!

Creamed Cabbage

1 medium head cabbage, shredded
½ cup salted boiling water
3 tablespoons butter
3 tablespoons flour
1½ cups milk
½ cup bread crumbs

Cook the cabbage in the water in a saucepan for 10 minutes. Drain and place the cabbage in a 2-quart baking dish. Melt the butter in a separate saucepan over a low heat; add the flour and stir until smooth. Add the milk, gradually, and stir until the mixture thickens. Pour the cream mixture over the cabbage. Top with the bread crumbs. Bake at 325 degrees for 15 minutes.

Traditional Cornbread Dressing

Two 14½-ounce cans chicken broth
8-inch skillet cornbread, cooked and crumbled
3 to 4 slices stale white bread, torn into pieces
1 medium onion, finely-chopped
2 celery stalks, finely-chopped
2 eggs, beaten
1 teaspoon sage
½ teaspoon salt
1 teaspoon pepper

Heat the chicken broth in a saucepan over a high heat to the boiling point. Remove the saucepan from heat. Combine the cornbread, bread pieces, onion and celery in a bowl. Add the eggs, sage, salt and pepper; mix well. Add the hot chicken broth and mix well. Place the mixture in a coated 9x13-inch baking dish. Bake at 300 degrees for 35 minutes or until light golden brown. Serve hot with turkey, chicken or ham.

Thunder 'n Lightning

3 medium tomatoes
1 large yellow or Vidalia onion, thinly sliced
2 large cucumbers, thinly sliced
14-ounce bottle Zesty Italian salad dressing
1 cup ice

Peel and core the tomatoes and cut into bite-size wedges. Place the tomatoes in a large container. Add the onion and cucumbers. Shake the bottle of dressing and pour over the vegetables. Stir to coat. Add the ice and stir to combine. Cover and chill for 2 hours. The ice will melt to thin the dressing. Stir before serving.

Serves 10 to 12.

This is a must, using summer vegetables.

Macaroni and Cheese à la Slow Cooker

16-ounce package macaroni
2 cups shredded sharp Cheddar cheese
Salt and pepper to taste
6 cups hot milk
1 stick butter

Cook the macaroni in water for 6 minutes in a saucepan and drain. Place 1 cup of the macaroni on the bottom of a heated slow cooker. Add 1 cup of the cheese and the salt and pepper. Add another layer of the macaroni and cheese. Pour in enough of the milk to cover. Cook on low for 5 hours or until thoroughly heated and the cheese is melted.

Baked Onions

2 dozen small white onions
⅓ cup butter, melted
1 tablespoon brown sugar
½ teaspoon salt
¼ teaspoon ground nutmeg
⅛ teaspoon red pepper
Dash of white pepper
¼ cup chopped almonds

Cook the onions in boiling water for 5 minutes. Drain and place the onions in a lightly coated 2-quart baking dish. Combine the butter, brown sugar, salt, nutmeg, red pepper and white pepper in a bowl. Drizzle the mixture over the onions and gently stir. Bake, covered, at 375 degrees for 45 minutes, stirring at 15 minute intervals. Sprinkle with the almonds.

Serves 6.

Fried Okra

2 eggs, beaten
¼ cup buttermilk
1 pound fresh okra, sliced
1 cup self-rising flour
1 cup self-rising cornmeal
Vegetable oil

Combine the eggs and buttermilk in a bowl. Add the okra and let stand for 10 minutes. Combine the flour and cornmeal. Drain the okra in small portions, using a slotted spoon. Dredge the okra, in small portions, in the flour mixture. Pour the oil to a depth of 2 to 3 inches into a heavy skillet. Fry the okra at 375 degrees until golden brown. Drain the okra and serve immediately.

Serves 4.

Oyster Casserole

8-ounce box oyster crackers
1 pint fresh oysters or two 8-ounce cans oysters
Salt and pepper to taste
2 eggs
2 cups milk
1 stick margarine

Crumble one layer of the crackers in the bottom of a coated 9x9-inch baking dish. Add a layer of the oysters and a dash of the salt and pepper. Add another thin layer of the crackers and a layer of the oysters and a final layer of the crackers. Season with the salt and pepper. Combine the liquid from the oysters and milk. Pour the mixture over the top of the casserole. Dot the top of the casserole with the margarine. Cover and chill for 12 hours. The casserole will look as if it has too much liquid. Chilling will allow the crackers to absorb the excess liquid. Bake at 350 degrees for 35 to 40 minutes.

Serves 4.

An unusual side dish— try it with beef or pork.

Bourbon Baked Peaches

4 peeled peach halves
4 tablespoons brown sugar
2 tablespoons butter
4 tablespoons Kentucky bourbon

Place the peaches in an 8x8-inch baking dish. Place equal parts of the brown sugar, butter and bourbon in each peach cavity. Bake at 325 degrees until the sauce is hot and bubbly.

Serves 4.

Beyond

Christmas Eve Family Gathering

Chicken Tetrazzini, page 115

Orange Almond Salad, page 74

Pickled Beets, page 129

Biscuits with Garlic, page 36

Bread Pudding and Bourbon Sauce, page 169

Merry Cranberry Crunch, page 167

Luscious and indulgent!

Decadent Chocolate Pound Cake

2½ cups flour
½ teaspoon salt
½ teaspoon baking soda
Six 1.55-ounce chocolate candy bars
2 sticks butter
2 cups sugar
4 eggs
1 cup buttermilk
2 teaspoons vanilla extract
1 cup chocolate sauce
Melted chocolate
Maraschino cherries

Sift the flour, salt and baking soda in a bowl. Melt the candy bars and butter in a saucepan. Add the sugar, eggs, buttermilk, vanilla extract and chocolate sauce. Add the chocolate mixture to the flour mixture; mix well. Pour the batter into a coated bundt pan. Bake at 350 degrees for 45 minutes or until done. Drizzle the top of the cake with the melted chocolate and garnish with the cherries.

Butter Rum Apple Cake

2 cups sugar
1½ cups oil
3 eggs
2 teaspoons rum extract
1 teaspoon vanilla extract
2 teaspoons cinnamon
½ teaspoon nutmeg
3 cups flour
1 teaspoon baking soda
½ teaspoon salt
4 cups peeled, finely-diced apples
1 cup chopped nuts
Powdered sugar, sifted

Combine the sugar and oil; mix well. Add the eggs, one at a time, beating well after each. Add the rum extract, vanilla extract, cinnamon and nutmeg. Sift the flour, baking soda and salt in a bowl. Add the flour mixture to the sugar mixture; mix well. Add the apples and nuts; stir well. Pour the stiff batter into a coated and floured tube or bundt pan. Bake at 350 degrees for 1½ hours. Allow the cake to cool and remove from the pan. Dust the cake with the powdered sugar. Freezes well.

Serves 16 to 20.

Kentucky Butter Cake

**2 sticks butter
2 cups sugar
4 eggs
1 cup buttermilk
2 teaspoons vanilla extract
3 cups flour, sifted**

Cream the butter and sugar in a large mixing bowl. Add the eggs, one at a time, beating well after each. Add the buttermilk and vanilla extract; stir well. Add the flour, gradually, stirring well. Turn the mixture into a coated 10-inch tube pan. Bake at 350 degrees for 1 hour. Remove the cake from the oven and cool. Run a spatula edge along the sides and prick the cake with a fork. Pour Kentucky Butter Cake Sauce over the cake. Allow to set 2 hours before serving.

Serves 8.

Kentucky Butter Cake Butter Sauce

**1 cup sugar
¼ cup water
½ cup butter
1 teaspoon rum extract**

Combine the sugar, water and butter in a saucepan. Heat until melted, but not boiling. Add the rum extract and remove the saucepan from the heat. Pour the sauce over the warm cake while the sauce is hot.

Chocolate Sauerkraut Cake

1½ cups sugar
⅔ cup shortening
3 eggs
1¼ teaspoons coconut flavoring
¼ teaspoon salt
½ cup cocoa
2¼ cups flour
1 teaspoon baking soda
1 teaspoon baking powder
1 cup water
⅔ cup sauerkraut, drained and rinsed

Cream the sugar and shortening in a bowl. Add the eggs and mix well. Add the coconut flavoring, salt and cocoa. Sift the flour, baking soda and baking powder in a bowl. Add the flour mixture and water to the shortening mixture. Fold in the sauerkraut. Pour the batter into a 9x13-inch cake pan. Do not overbake. Use your favorite chocolate icing.

For a quick cake use a chocolate cake mix. Add the sauerkraut and coconut flavoring and bake as directed in the recipe.

Flavor is enhanced if prepared up to two days in advance.

Orange Bundt Cake

18¼-ounce box yellow cake mix
½ cup margarine
½ cup orange juice
½ cup water
½ cup vegetable oil
3-ounce package vanilla instant pudding mix
4 eggs

Combine the cake mix, margarine, orange juice, water, oil, pudding mix and eggs in a bowl; mix well. Pour the batter into a coated bundt pan. Bake at 350 degrees for 30 minutes. Cover with the Orange Bundt Cake Glaze.

Orange Bundt Cake Glaze

½ cup orange juice
½ cup margarine
1 cup sugar

Combine the orange juice, margarine and sugar in a saucepan. Bring the mixture to a boil and boil for 3 minutes. Poke holes in the cake using a wooden pick. Pour the glaze over the cake and let stand for 20 minutes.

Praline Cheesecake

1½ pounds cream cheese, at room temperature
2 cups brown sugar
3 eggs
2 tablespoons self-rising flour
2 teaspoons vanilla extract
½ cup chopped pecans
1 cup graham cracker crumbs
3 tablespoons sugar
3 tablespoons butter

Combine the cream cheese and brown sugar; mix well. Add the eggs, flour, vanilla extract and pecans. Combine the graham cracker crumbs, sugar and butter in a separate bowl to form a crust. Pat the mixture into a 10-inch springform pan. Pour the cream cheese mixture into the crust. Bake at 350 degrees for 35 minutes.

So simple to make yet this dessert will get rave reviews!

Sour Cream Chocolate Cheesecake

2 cups graham cracker crumbs
3 tablespoons sugar
⅓ cup melted margarine
2 eggs
½ cup sugar
2 teaspoons vanilla extract
1½ cups sour cream
Two 8-ounce packages cream cheese
2 tablespoons melted margarine
8 ounces semisweet chocolate chips, melted

Combine the crumbs, the 3 tablespoons of sugar and the ⅓ cup of margarine in a bowl; mix well. Pat the mixture into the bottom of a springform pan. Bake at 325 degrees for 8 minutes. Remove and cool. Combine the eggs, the ½ cup of sugar, vanilla extract and sour cream in a blender container; process. Remove the cover and add the cream cheese, one chunk at a time, with the motor running. Add the 2 tablespoons margarine and chocolate chips after the cheese is blended; blend again. Pour the mixture into the crust. Bake at 350 degrees for 40 minutes.

Chocolate Chip Cheesecake

16 ounces cream cheese, at room temperature
⅓ cup sugar
1 tablespoon vanilla extract
34 ounces chocolate chip cookie dough

Combine the cream cheese, sugar and vanilla extract in a bowl with an electric mixer until creamy and smooth. Slice the cookie dough. Pat ½ of the slices into the bottom of a pie pan. Smooth the cream cheese mixture on top of the dough. Pat the remaining slices in your hands and place on the top, covering the entire pan. Bake at 350 degrees for 15 minutes or until golden brown.. Let cool. Serve at room temperature or chilled.

A cheesecake for kids of all ages.

Kentucky Chocolate Bourbon Balls

½ cup softened butter
1-pound box powdered sugar
¼ cup Kentucky bourbon
1 cup chopped pecans
Four 1-ounce squares semisweet chocolate
Four 1-ounce squares unsweetened chocolate
Pecan halves

Cream the butter and gradually add the powdered sugar, beating with an electric mixer at a medium speed. Add the bourbon and beat until smooth. Stir in the pecans. Shape the dough into 1-inch balls. Cover the balls and chill for 8 hours. Combine the squares of chocolate in the top of a double boiler. Reduce the heat to low and cook, stirring often, until the chocolate melts. Pierce with a wooden pick and dip each ball in the chocolate. Place the balls on waxed paper. Gently press a pecan half on top of each ball. Chill until the chocolate hardens.

Makes about 48 balls.

Chocolate Mint Kisses

2 egg whites
¾ cup sugar
½ teaspoon peppermint extract
2 drops green food coloring
6-ounce package chocolate chips

Beat the egg whites with an electric mixer until stiff, gradually adding the sugar. Add the peppermint extract and food coloring. Stir in the chocolate chips. Drop the mixture by heaping spoonfuls onto an uncoated baking sheet. Place in a preheated oven at 350 degrees and turn off the oven. Allow the Kisses to remain in the closed oven for 8 hours. Remove and store in an airtight container.

Noodle Clusters

12-ounce package semisweet chocolate chips
1 cup peanuts
3½ cups chow mein noodles
½ cup raisins

Melt the chocolate chips in the top of a double boiler. Remove from the heat. Stir in the peanuts, chow mein noodles and raisins. Drop the mixture by heaping spoonfuls onto waxed paper. Cool and store in an airtight container.

Makes 2 to 3 dozen clusters.

Caramel or butterscotch pieces can be used in place of the chocolate chips.

Friday Fudge

12-ounce bag semisweet chocolate chips
16-ounce can chocolate cake frosting
½ cup chopped nuts

Melt the chocolate chips in a bowl in the microwave, stirring to smooth. Combine the melted chocolate and frosting in a bowl. Add the nuts and stir. Pour the fudge into a buttered glass dish. Allow the fudge to set before cutting into squares.

A super easy, smooth fudge, without the stirring!

Easy Peanut Brittle

**2 cups sugar
1 cup light corn syrup
1 cup water
2 cups unroasted peanuts
¼ teaspoon salt
1 teaspoon butter
1 teaspoon soda
1 teaspoon vanilla extract**

Combine the sugar, corn syrup and water in a saucepan. Cook to 236 degrees on a candy thermometer. Add the peanuts and salt; cook to 295 degrees or hard crack stage. Remove the saucepan from the heat and immediately add the butter, soda and vanilla extract, stirring constantly. Pour the mixture into a coated 9x13-inch baking sheet. Allow the brittle to harden.

Buckeye Balls

**16-ounce jar creamy peanut butter
1 cup butter or margarine, softened
16-ounce package powdered sugar
12-ounce package chocolate chips
2 tablespoons shortening**

Combine the peanut butter and butter in a bowl. Beat with an electric mixture on a medium speed until blended. Add the powdered sugar, gradually, beating until blended. Shape the mixture into 1-inch balls. Chill for 10 minutes or until the dough is firm. Microwave the chocolate chips and shortening in a 2-quart baking dish for 1½ minutes or until melted, stirring twice. Dip each ball using a wooden pick into the melted chocolate until partially coated. Place the balls on waxed paper to set. Store the balls in an airtight container.

Makes 7 dozen balls.

Brown Sugar Cookies

2 cups brown sugar
1 cup shortening
2 eggs
½ cup sour milk
3½ cups sifted flour
1 teaspoon baking soda
1 teaspoon salt
½ cup nuts

Combine the sugar, shortening and eggs in a bowl and mix well. Stir in the milk. Sift the flour, baking soda and salt in a bowl. Stir the flour mixture into the batter. Add the nuts. Drop by teaspoonfuls onto a baking sheet. Bake at 350 degrees for 10 to 12 minutes. Frost with a powdered sugar icing when the cookies are cool.

Chocolate Crackle Cookies

¾ cup cocoa
⅔ cup oil
2 cups sugar
4 eggs
2 teaspoons vanilla extract
2 cups flour
½ teaspoon salt
2 teaspoons baking powder
Powdered sugar

Combine the cocoa, oil, sugar, eggs, vanilla extract, flour, salt and baking powder in a bowl; mix well. Form the dough into balls. Put the powdered sugar in a bowl. Roll the balls in the powdered sugar. Place the cookies on a baking sheet. Bake at 350 degrees for 10 to 12 minutes.

Fastest Ever Chocolate Chip Cookies

2 sticks margarine
1½ cups brown sugar
2 eggs
1 teaspoon vanilla extract
1 teaspoon baking soda
2¼ cups self-rising flour
8 ounces chocolate chips

Melt the margarine on a baking sheet in the oven. Cream the brown sugar and eggs. Add the vanilla extract and baking soda. Add the melted margarine. Add 1½ cups of the flour and mix well. Add the remaining flour and mix well. Add the chocolate chips and mix well. Spread the mixture onto the baking sheet and bake at 350 degrees for 10 minutes or until light brown. Cool and cut into squares.

Santa's Favorite Molasses Cookies

¾ cup shortening
¼ cup molasses
1 cup sugar
1 egg
2 cups flour
2 teaspoons baking soda
½ teaspoon salt
½ teaspoon cloves
½ teaspoon ginger
1 teaspoon cinnamon
Granulated sugar

Melt the shortening in a saucepan over a low heat. Remove the saucepan from the heat and allow the shortening to cool. Add the molasses, sugar and egg; beat well. Sift the flour, soda, salt, cloves, ginger and cinnamon in a bowl. Add the flour mixture to the molasses mixture and mix well. Wrap the dough in plastic wrap and chill overnight. Form the dough into 1-inch balls and roll each ball in the granulated sugar. Place the cookies on a lightly-coated baking sheet and bake at 350 degrees for 8 to 10 minutes. Cool before serving.

Million Dollar Cookies

1 cup butter
1 cup brown sugar
1 cup sugar
2 eggs
1 teaspoon vanilla extract
2½ cups oats
2 cups flour
½ teaspoon salt
1 teaspoon baking powder
1 teaspoon baking soda
4-ounce chocolate candy bar
12-ounce package chocolate chips
1½ cups chopped nuts

Cream the butter, brown sugar and sugar in a bowl. Stir in the eggs and vanilla extract. Grind the oats in a blender container until fine. Add the oats, flour, salt, baking powder and baking soda. Grate the candy bar in the blender container. Add the grated chocolate, chocolate chips and nuts; mix well. Drop the dough by spoonfuls, 2 inches apart, on to a coated baking sheet. Bake at 375 degrees for 10 minutes.

Makes 55 cookies.

These make great cookies for a gift basket.

Lemon Bars

2 sticks butter, at room temperature
2 cups flour
½ cup powdered sugar
4 beaten eggs
2 cups sugar
4 tablespoons flour
4 tablespoons lemon juice
Powdered sugar

Combine the butter, the 2 cups of flour and powdered sugar in a bowl; blend well. Press the mixture into a 9x13-inch baking dish. Bake the crust at 325 degrees for 20 minutes. Combine the eggs, sugar, the 4 tablespoons of flour and lemon juice; blend well. Pour the mixture over the cooked crust. Return to the oven and bake for 20 minutes. Cut into bars and sift the powdered sugar over the top while warm.

Pumpkin Bars

2 cups flour
2 cups sugar
2 teaspoons baking powder
1 teaspoon baking soda
¼ teaspoon salt
2 teaspoons cinnamon
½ teaspoon nutmeg
½ teaspoon ginger
¼ teaspoon cloves
1 cup salad oil
4 eggs
2 cups canned pumpkin
1-pound box powdered sugar
Two 3-ounce packages cream cheese, at room temperature
1 tablespoon milk
2 teaspoons vanilla extract

These make a nice addition or alternative to pumpkin pie.

⅓ cup melted butter
½ teaspoon cream of tartar

Combine the flour, sugar, baking powder, baking soda, salt, cinnamon, nutmeg, ginger and cloves in a bowl. Add the oil, eggs and pumpkin; mix well. Pour the mixture into 10x15-inch baking dish. Bake at 350 degrees for 20 minutes. Set aside to cool. Combine the powdered sugar, cream cheese, milk, vanilla extract, butter and cream of tartar in a large bowl. Beat until the mixture is creamy and smooth. Spread the cream cheese mixture over the top of the baked portion. Cut into bars and serve.

Serves 18.

Chocolate Marshmallow Bars

½ cup shortening
1 cup sugar
1 egg
2 eggs, separated
1½ cups flour
1 teaspoon baking powder
¼ teaspoon salt
1 cup nuts
½ cup semisweet chocolate chips
1 cup miniature marshmallows
1 cup packed light brown sugar

Cream the shortening and sugar with an electric mixer. Beat in the egg and 2 egg yolks. Sift the flour, baking powder and salt in a bowl. Add the flour mixture to the egg mixture and mix well. Spread the batter in a 9x13-inch baking dish. Sprinkle the nuts, chocolate chips and marshmallows over the batter. Beat the 2 egg whites until stiff. Fold the brown sugar into the egg whites. Spread the egg white mixture over the batter. Bake at 350 degrees for 30 to 40 minutes. Cut into bars. Serve warm or cooled.

Makes 32 bars.

Chess Squares

1 stick margarine, melted
4 eggs
18¼-ounce box yellow cake mix
8-ounce package cream cheese, at room temperature
1-pound box powdered sugar

Combine the margarine, 1 of the eggs and cake mix. Press the mixture into the bottom of a 9x13-inch baking dish. Combine the cream cheese, the remaining 3 eggs and powdered sugar. Pour the mixture over the crust. Bake at 350 degrees for 35 to 40 minutes.

Variations:
Use a chocolate cake mix and 2 teaspoons of cocoa;
a lemon cake mix and sprinkle with powdered sugar or add 1 cup chopped nuts.

Taste rich and delicious. Kids will love them!

Speedy Little Devils

18¾-ounce box devil's food cake mix
1 stick butter or margarine, melted
½ cup creamy peanut butter
7 or 7½-ounce jar marshmallow creme

Combine the cake mix and butter. Reserve 1½ cups of the mixture for the top. Pat the remaining crumb mixture into the bottom of a 9x13-inch baking dish. Combine the peanut butter and marshmallow creme in a bowl. Spread the mixture evenly over the crust. Crumble the reserved crumb mixture over the top. Bake at 350 degrees for 20 minutes. Cool and cut into bars.

Easy Pie Crust

1 cup self-rising flour
⅓ cup cooking oil
3 tablespoons milk

Combine the flour, oil and milk in a 9-inch pie pan. Mix with a fork to form a dough. Press the dough into the pie pan with your fingers. Prick the crust with a fork. Bake at 350 degrees for 3 to 4 minutes to set for recipes that use a baked crust.

Peanut Butter Pie

1 cup powdered sugar
½ cup peanut butter
9-inch baked piecrust
¼ cup cornstarch
⅔ cup sugar
¼ teaspoon salt
2 cups milk
3 egg yolks, beaten
2 tablespoons butter
¼ teaspoon vanilla extract
3 egg whites

Combine the powdered sugar and peanut butter in a bowl with a fork until well blended. Spread ⅔ of this mixture into the piecrust. Combine the cornstarch, sugar, salt, milk, egg yolks, butter and vanilla extract in a saucepan. Cook until thick, like custard. Set aside to cool. Pour the cooled custard mixture over the peanut butter mixture. Beat the egg whites into a smooth meringue. Spread the meringue over the custard mixture. Sprinkle the remaining peanut butter mixture on top of the meringue. Bake at 300 degrees for 20 to 25 minutes or until meringue is firm and golden brown.

Serves 6.

This is our all-time favorite from cousin Betty. Anyone can make this crust.

Pecan Pie

¼ cup butter
⅔ cup firmly-packed brown sugar
¼ teaspoon salt
¾ cup dark corn syrup
3 eggs, beaten
1 teaspoon vanilla extract
1 cup pecan halves
9-inch unbaked piecrust

Cream the butter and brown sugar until fluffy. Add the salt, corn syrup, eggs and vanilla extract. Place the pecan halves into the piecrust. Pour the filling over the pecans. Bake at 450 degrees for 10 minutes; reduce the heat to 350 degrees and bake for 35 minutes or until a knife inserted comes out clean.

Makes one pie.

Cherry-O-Cream Cheese Pie

8-ounce package cream cheese, at room temperature
14-ounce can sweetened condensed milk
⅓ cup lemon juice
1 teaspoon vanilla extract
9-inch crumb crust or baked piecrust
21-ounce can cherry pie filling

Whip the cream cheese with an electric mixer until fluffy. Add the sweetened condensed milk, gradually, and continue to beat until well blended. Add the lemon juice and vanilla extract, blending well. Pour the mixture into the crust. Chill for 2 to 3 hours. Spread the pie filling evenly over the cream cheese mixture and chill.

Peaches 'n Cream Pie

1 cup sugar
8-ounce package cream cheese, at room temperature
8-ounce container whipped topping, at room temperature
3 to 4 large fresh peaches, peeled and pitted
1 graham cracker piecrust

Combine the sugar and cream cheese in a bowl. Cream with an electric mixer on a high speed. Stir in the whipped topping and mix at a low speed until well blended. Cut the peaches into bite-size pieces. Layer the peaches in the bottom of the crust. Pour the cream mixture on top of the peaches spreading evenly to cover. Cover and chill overnight. The pie may also be frozen; thaw before serving.

This is a light, refreshing summer dessert, which can be made with reduced-fat crust, cream cheese and whipped topping. Caution: do not use fat-free cream cheese because it will not blend well with the sugar.

Lemon Pie Update

6-ounce package sugar-free/fat-free vanilla instant pudding mix
1 individual tub Crystal Light lemonade mix
2 cups skim milk
12-ounce carton non-fat whipped topping
1 graham cracker piecrust

Combine the pudding mix, lemonade, skim milk and whipped topping with an electric mixer in a large bowl; beat well. Pour into the crust. Chill until ready to serve.

Summertime Peach Pie

1 egg
⅓ cup melted margarine
⅓ cup self-rising flour
1 cup sugar
1 teaspoon vanilla extract
3 to 4 fresh peaches, sliced or 16-ounce can sliced peaches, drained
9-inch unbaked piecrust

Combine the egg, margarine, flour, sugar and vanilla extract in a bowl; mix well. Place the peaches in the bottom of piecrust. Pour the egg mixture over the peaches. Bake at 350 degrees for 1 hour or until brown.

Mmmm!
Try this
instead of
cobbler.
Great dish.

Run for the Roses Pie

3 eggs, slightly beaten
1 cup light corn syrup
1 cup sugar
1 tablespoon melted margarine
1 teaspoon vanilla extract
2 tablespoons Kentucky bourbon
1 cup pecan halves
6 ounces semisweet chocolate chips
9-inch unbaked pie crust

Combine the eggs, syrup, sugar, margarine, vanilla extract and bourbon in a bowl; stir well. Add the pecans and chocolate chips; mix well. Pour the mixture into the piecrust. Place the pie on a baking sheet and bake at 350 degrees for 45 minutes or until the top is golden brown.

Serves 8.

*An old
standard and
an all-time
favorite!*

Dried Apple Pies

4 cups dried apples
1 cup sugar
½ teaspoon nutmeg
½ teaspoon cinnamon
½ teaspoon allspice
½ teaspoon cloves
2 cups self-rising flour
½ cup shortening
Milk
Oil

Cook the apples in enough water to cover in a heavy saucepan for 45 minutes or until the apples are tender; drain. Add the sugar, nutmeg, cinnamon, allspice and cloves. Combine the flour and shortening in a bowl; mix well. Add enough of the milk to make a stiff batter. Roll the dough out on a floured board and cut into six circles. Place one heaping tablespoon of the apples in the center of each circle and fold over. Crimp the edges with a fork. Poke holes in the top with the fork. Fry the pies in a heavy iron skillet in ½ inch of the oil. Remove and place on paper towels to drain.

Merry Cranberry Crunch

2 cups rolled oats
1 cup flour
2 cups brown sugar
1 cup butter or margarine
2 cups whole-berry cranberry sauce
½ cup chopped nuts

Blend the oats, flour, brown sugar and butter until crumbly. Pour ½ of the oat mixture into a coated 9x13-inch baking dish. Pour the cranberry sauce over the oat mixture. Spread the remaining oat mixture on top. Sprinkle the nuts on top. Bake at 350 degrees for 45 minutes. Serve warm topped with ice cream or whipped topping.

Serves 8 to 10.

A
fall delight!

Pumpkin Dessert

16-ounce can mashed pumpkin
4 eggs
5-ounce can evaporated milk
1½ cups sugar
2 teaspoons cinnamon
1 teaspoon ginger
½ teaspoon nutmeg
18¼-ounce box yellow cake mix
2 sticks butter, melted
Chopped walnuts

Combine the pumpkin, eggs, evaporated milk, sugar, cinnamon, ginger and nutmeg in a bowl; mix well. Pour the mixture into a 9x13-inch baking dish. Sprinkle the cake mix evenly over the pumpkin mixture. Drizzle the butter on top and sprinkle with the nuts. Bake at 350 degrees for 1 hour. Serve chilled with whipped cream.

Serves 16 to 20.

Bread Pudding and Bourbon Sauce

1 loaf day-old bread, cubed
Two 10-ounce cans evaporated milk
¼ teaspoon nutmeg
Dash of cinnamon
6 eggs
¾ cup brown sugar
⅓ cup raisins
2 tablespoons vanilla extract

Place the bread cubes into a lightly-coated 3-quart baking dish. Warm the milk slowly in a saucepan, without boiling. Add the nutmeg and cinnamon, stirring to blend. Whip the eggs in a separate bowl. Add the brown sugar and mix well. Slowly add the warm milk mixture to the eggs. Stir in the raisins and vanilla extract. Pour the mixture over the bread cubes. Lightly press with the back of a spoon to moisten. Bake at 300 degrees for 50 minutes. Serve warm with Bourbon Sauce.

Bourbon Sauce

1 cup sugar
4 tablespoons butter
½ cup dark corn syrup
21-ounce can cherry pie filling
⅓ cup Kentucky bourbon

Melt the sugar and butter in the top of a double boiler. Add the corn syrup and mix well. Remove the saucepan from the heat. Stir in the pie filling and bourbon. Serve warm, spooned over Bread Pudding.

Cherries in the Snow

1½ sticks margarine, melted
1½ cups flour
2 tablespoons sugar
¾ cup chopped pecans
11 ounces cream cheese, at room temperature
3 cups powdered sugar
12-ounce carton whipped topping
21-ounce can cherry pie filling

Combine the margarine, flour, sugar and pecans until stiff. Press the mixture into a 9x13-inch baking dish. Bake at 350 degrees for 25 minutes or until brown. Combine the cream cheese, powdered sugar and whipped topping; mix until smooth. Spread over the cooled crust. Top with the pie filling. Chill and serve.

Apple Cobbler

2 pounds quartered apples
3 tablespoons butter
1¼ cups sugar, divided
¼ teaspoon cinnamon
⅛ teaspoon nutmeg
1 stick butter, melted
1 cup flour
2 teaspoons baking powder
1 teaspoon salt
½ cup milk

Sauté the apples in the 3 tablespoons of butter in a skillet until tender. Add ¼ cup of the sugar, cinnamon and nutmeg; stir. Pour the melted butter into a 9x13-inch baking dish. Combine the remaining 1 cup of sugar, flour, baking powder and salt; mix well. Stir in the milk. Pour the batter in the baking dish. Add the apples. Bake at 350 degrees for 50 to 60 minutes or until the crust is a toasted brown.

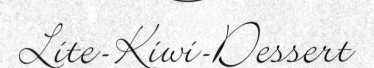

Lite-Kiwi-Dessert

10 ounce angel food cake, torn into bite-size pieces
6 peeled kiwi, sliced
3 large bananas, sliced
1 quart fresh strawberries, sliced
6-ounce box fat-free sugar-free vanilla instant pudding mix
16-ounce container whipped topping

Layer the cake, kiwi, bananas and strawberries in a large glass bowl. Prepare the pudding according to the package directions. Beat in the whipped topping. Pour the pudding mixture over the fruit and chill. Garnish with extra kiwi and strawberry slices.

Blackberry Sherbet

1 pint fresh blackberries, washed and picked over
½ cup honey
½ cup evaporated milk
2 tablespoons lemon juice

Combine the blackberries, honey, evaporated milk and lemon juice in a blender container and process until smooth. Pour the mixture into an ice cream freezer and freeze according to the manufacturer's directions.

Makes 2 pints.

Lemon Ice Cream

1 cup whole milk
1 scant cup sugar
Juice of 2 lemons
Finely-grated rind of 1 lemon
1 cup whipping cream

Warm the milk in a saucepan over a medium-low heat just until it's hot–do not let it boil or scald. Add the sugar, stirring until the sugar dissolves. Remove the saucepan from the heat and allow the mixture cool. Cover and chill. Add the lemon juice, rind and whipping cream and stir. Freeze according to the ice cream maker's instructions.

Makes 1 quart.

Praline Sauce

1½ cups light corn syrup
½ cup heavy cream
2 tablespoons butter
2 cups pecan halves, lightly toasted
2 teaspoons vanilla extract

Combine the corn syrup, cream and butter in a saucepan; mix well. Bring the mixture to a boil over a medium heat, stirring constantly. Boil for 2 minutes and remove from the heat. Add the pecans and vanilla extract; stir well. Allow the sauce to cool. Store the sauce in a tightly covered container in the refrigerator. Serve the sauce hot or cold over ice cream. Heat the sauce over a low heat until it's pourable.

Makes about 2½ cups.

Fresh fruit—especially sliced peaches and strawberries—are delicious with this super-cooling ice cream. It's wonderfully creamy, but also has that lemon tartness to balance its rich flavor. This recipe is for a 1-quart churn.

Index